5

NECESSARY
SKILLS

To Keep Your Career On Track

Funded by
MISSION COLLEGE

Carl D. Perkins Vocational and Technical Education Act Grant

5

NECESSARY
SKILLS
To Keep Your Career On Track

Richard S. Pearson

Outskirts Press, Inc.
Denver, Colorado

5 Necessary Skills To Keep Your Career On Track
Recession Proof Guidance for How to Negotiate a Job Offer, Conduct Job Interviews, Interview Questions, Career Changes, Job Searches, Cover Letters, Resumes, Mentoring, Dealing With Bad Managers, Networking Tools, and the Answers to Other Work-Related Questions, Including "Laid Off! Now What?"

Outskirts Press, Inc.
http://www.outskirtspress.com

ISBN: 978-1-4327-4137-2

Library of Congress Control Number: 2009927232

Outskirts Press and the "OP" logo are trademarks belonging to Outskirts Press, Inc.

PRINTED IN THE UNITED STATES OF AMERICA

"Being prepared for the twists and turns and disappointments of today's job market means we have to take control of our lives and gain knowledge about how to handle them."

Carol Kleiman – Author of *Winning the Job Game: The New Rules for Finding and Keeping the Job You Want*

Do something you love to do and
you will never work a day in your life.
Confucius

TABLE OF CONTENTS

INTRODUCTION

Careers must be planned, nurtured and directed to be successful, life-long endeavors. Employment, as we have known it in this country and much of the western world, is going through pronounced change – the transformation accelerated by technological developments and the impact of the Great Recession. This book will go through the long-term trend away from the traditional employer-employee relationship to a contingent workforce and the profound impact this will have on the way you go about managing your career going forward. It will explore the concept of "job security," as it applies to careers of the future.

The philosopher and poet, Dante writes in the 12th Century: The secret of getting things done is to act! This is the same lesson carried forward by Stephen R. Covey in many of his books - what he coins as proactivity. You, and only you, are ultimately responsible for your career. To leave something this important in the hands of a manager, company, union, school or anybody else—or to only react to circumstances that befall you—can be a mistake of a life time. The best advice in the world won't do you any good unless you take the information and proactively do something with it.

Social media has had a profound change on how people interact and network. This, along with new technology and communication devices, has facilitated major shifts in the way we go about finding, applying for, and keeping jobs, as well as staying in contact with friends and colleagues. Networking is critical to secure your employment going forward – both to be in the "know" about potential changes in your job and industry and to stay a step ahead of the game in maintaining your own career. Marketing, customer service, consumer knowledge and product choice are going through dramatic transformations brought about by social media.

Developing mindfulness of all your surroundings and the environment where you live and work is of utmost importance. This includes not only your co-workers next door or your boss in the corner office, but also your company, trade, products, competitors, and the general health of the local and national economy. This will make you a more knowledgeable and useful employee and give you the insight to better position yourself and your company and its' products in the marketplace, as well as help you make any (necessary) career choices. Being proactive will assist in all of your business and career endeavors, whether it's getting a report out on time, contemplating your customer's needs, or implementing a beneficial, new process before your boss mandates it. It's recognizing changes in your industry or organization that aren't "positive" for you personally - and to start the process to either adapt or make a job change, on your terms and timetable. It is to be continually educated and re-educated in your chosen profession, and the economic and geopolitical outlook in general. If you are not gaining knowledge on new and changing processes you are losing your competitive edge to contemporaries.

Learning to deal with many management styles and degrees of professionalism (or lack thereof) will give you an advantage over your co-workers. You need to develop honest and straightforward dialog with bosses, so you know their expectations. Getting along with other employees in your workplace, recognizing cultural differences and unique work styles, and keeping communications open and positive will be a huge boost to personal career development. Complex jobs, especially in the periods of economic downturn where additional tasks were handed to the survivors, have made it critical to work well with others to get projects completed.

You don't have to go through your career planning, execution and development on your own. Career coaches can add outside perspective, and you will definitely want to develop mentor relationships to help guide you along your chosen path. Give back to others and mentor those who can gain advantage of your knowledge and experience. Create a network with industry colleagues, old college friends, professional associations, church groups, and others to keep you abreast of changes in your industry and up-to-date knowledge of the job market, to improve your marketability.

The imperative message of this book is that you are ultimately responsible for your life and life's work. How well you prepare yourself for, and adapt to, "change" will determine your success. Your preparedness will be your only job security in the future.

CHAPTER 1

The Future of Jobs

"Business is like riding a bicycle.
Either you keep moving or you fall down."
Frank Lloyd Wright

The same thing can be said about jobs. You must keep moving forward (progressing, learning, collaborating) or you are actually falling backward, as the world passes by. The first edition of *5 Necessary Skills to Keep Your Career on Track* went through many of the painful details of how we landed in what has been termed the "Great Recession" and how it has accelerated changes in employment. This new edition focuses on helping to craft the mindset necessary to maintain continuous employment given the new workplace environment and how we communicate, how companies recruit and hire, your ability to adapt and change, and comprehend the very nature of the jobs you will hold going forward.

In the second decade of the *two-thousands* and beyond,

there will be no return to the "customary" jobs market and "traditional" exit from recessions. In the past, we could always depend on the creation of new small businesses to pull us bootstrapping out of recessions. After all, this entrepreneurial segment generated more than two-thirds of all new jobs in the past two decades. But there was a perfect storm against us this time: the lost decade of the stock market, the housing bubble burst and corresponding loss of personal wealth, and the deepest recession of (most) of our lifetimes. These conditions have reduced risk-taking as workers are postponing retirement, trying to replenish savings accounts, and scrimping to fund their children's college education. Coupled with the unwillingness of the banking industry to fund startup operations, the small business pathway to success is all but stymied for entrepreneurs. We can only be hopeful this segment will again become the jobs "engine."

The government, despite its intent, is not really doing much to better the situation. We, as a country, cannot continue spending fifty percent more than the tax revenue taken in - just as families cannot overspend their monthly incomes for long. The day to "pay the piper" will come. Foreign governments and businesses will not continue to feed the "black hole" called the US National Debt. Therefore, the government will not be able to flood the market with stimulus dollars in the future (nor have these programs created anywhere near the number of jobs projected). Net, net, the jobs market will never be quite the same. The US is being outgunned in several key technology areas, such as supercomputing, lithium ion batteries (for electric cars), and nanotechnology by China, Japan, and South Korean. Our government must strive to regain our national leadership position in research and development to get back on top technologically. And do all in its power to advance educational incentives for math and sciences to prepare our coming generations for the future.

Professor Charles Handy, in *The Age of Unreason*, predicted a few decades ago that just after the turn of the century less than half the work force in the industrialized world would be in "proper" full-time jobs in organizations. He was writing about the traditional employer/employee relationship. If you add up the unemployed/fallen off benefits/given up looking, part-time, sole proprietors, temporary and contract workers, and stay-at-home parents it equals over one-half of the 153 million US workforce. Professor Handy was right on target. This trend will continue away from the traditional employer/employee relationship. We already see virtual multimillion-dollar corporations, with a half-dozen employees – the bulk of their businesses outsourced to other firms or individuals. Corporations for decades have outsourced legal, advertising, marketing, logistics, facilities, accounting, etc. – but now everything is on the table, even R&D, manufacturing, design, and sales – no business process or function is considered sacred. Much of this outsourcing had given rise to the increasing number of small business startups, as recipients, during periods of economic growth. But when times are tough, these functions are trimmed back as well.

Telecommuting is racing forward, with virtual call centers replacing expensive facilities, and various "specialist" professionals able to collaborate from remote locations. The technological advancements making this possible have also leveled the playing field for countries and international businesses. Chinese and Indian graduates of US and UK universities, with advanced degrees, no longer have to stay in those countries for good jobs. They can go back home and work for businesses anywhere in the world, with all the latest "tools" at their disposal. Besides the advantage of many workers not having to commute or get displaced from their homelands, a big benefit is flexible hours—which is so important for those raising families or continuing their education.

We have also seen an unprecedented number of people delaying their retirement plans because of the loss of the equity in their homes, 401K plans, or other investments. This compounds the problem of the lack of new jobs being created, as they are occupying positions that younger workers would have traditionally filled.

Where does this leave the American worker? How should he or she prepare for the future? Where will job security come from and how will they support their families going forward in the lifestyle they experienced? Economists see jobs growth (when it begins in earnest) to fit into two roughly equal categories: High-end professionals/specialists and low skill-low wage positions. The highly trained professionals, such as network engineers, doctors, software designers, and low-end, such as retail clerks and health care aids, leave a big gap in the middle. These moderate paying jobs, which include real estate sales, office administrators, factory supervisors, construction foreman, etc. may not come back in significant numbers this decade. People who have been displaced from these mid-level jobs are either going to have to accept lower paying service positions or be re-trained and re-educated to become "specialists" in their fields. This is not to say all of these moderate pay jobs are going away – there just won't be growth in this segment. You must also get in the mindset that it is okay to work as a contingent worker on contract or temporary assignment. And get weaned off the dependence of the bi-weekly paycheck and benefits package offered to traditional full-time employees, because of the lack of growth in this mid-level segment and the fact that you just might be working for yourself. More and more firms are reluctant to hire large, permanent workforces because of doubts about the long-term durability of the economy—and precipitous swings in business cycles. And it can be easier and less costly to outsource a particular function than to assume the risks and start it in house. Currently there are 19 million self-employed or sole proprietors in the country and this number will continue climbing, as will small businesses of 2 to 499 workers (as we come out of the post-recession doldrums). Large and medium-sized companies (500+ employees) will remain stagnant, in the aggregate, in total workforce numbers.

All workers should do a regular and thorough analysis of their skills - those mastered during their career so far - because that is what companies will be looking for, not the job titles held, for both employees and contingent workers. These skills must be highlighted on your resume and align closely with the position requirements of the prospective job - backed up by the functions you have mastered and your education. Regarding education, it is a never-ending process. (The analogy the chapter opened with applies: you stop moving on a bicycle and you fall over.) You have got to show your employer that you thirst for knowledge. Demonstrate you are regularly adding educational experiences and contributing to innovation in the workplace. Business models change. New competition and product evolution occurs and you must exhibit your ability to change, to be flexible, to collaborate with team members, and contribute to meet whatever new demand befalls the organization. Management is looking for people with creative ways to solve existing problems. People who will progress to higher levels in organizations are the ones who develop and use exceptional conflict resolution skills. They cannot come across as temperamental or unyielding no matter how creative they are. If you are not gaining knowledge and progressing in your field - simply maintaining the status quo - you are slowly sliding backwards. You risk loosing ground to co-workers and competitors and becoming less relevant. Seize every opportunity for additional training and take courses to broaden your perspective. Become an expert in something(s) and plan for your future, whether it is to start your own business or consultancy someday, or just to be the best you can be as an employee or contractor for a company.

Life long employment of generations ago was replaced by baby boomers with 3-5 jobs over their careers. Now Generation X (it is projected) will hold 10-15 and the Generation Y 25+ jobs over their working years. Therefore, it is of utmost importance for these latter generations to have continuously updated skills to land that next job – because they will be, in effect, continuously looking.

Back to a simpler time—before FedEx worldwide delivery, Skype, or text messaging—before globalization, different values were shaped and mindsets were formed that baby boomers carried into the workplace, both as workers and leaders of companies. There was little worry about what went on in the office after 5 p.m. Layoffs for white-collar workers were almost unheard of. As children, we took for granted that if we paid our dues and got a good education, we could expect to be better off than our parents.

In this era, we learned what it was to work hard and

build self-esteem. Randy Pausch writes about the importance of this in *The Last Lecture* and comments that many kids today are missing these important lessons of life. How will they be prepared for the new economics and changing business environment – to be confident enough in themselves to face the challenges of the American workplace?

There's a lot of talk these days about giving children self-esteem. It's not something you can give; it's something they have to build. Coach Graham worked in a no-coddling zone. Self-esteem? He knew there was really only one way to teach kids how to develop it: You give them something they can't do, they work hard until they find they can do it, and you just keep repeating the process.

I realize that, these days, a guy like Coach Graham might get thrown out of a youth sports league. He'd be too tough. Parents would complain.

I remember one game when our team was playing terribly. At halftime, in our rush for water, we almost knocked over the water bucket. Coach Graham was livid: "Jeez! That's the most I've seen you boys move since this game started!" We were eleven years old, just standing there, afraid he'd pick us up one by one and break us with his bare hands. "Water?" He barked. "You boys want water?" He lifted the bucket and dumped all the water on the ground.

We watched him walk away and heard him mutter to an assistant coach: "You can give water to the first-string defense. They played OK."

Now let me be clear: Coach Graham would never endanger any kid. One reason he worked so hard on conditioning was he knew it reduces injuries. However, it was a chilly day, we'd all had access to water during the first half, and the dash to the water bucket was more about us being a bunch of brats than really needing hydration.

Even so, if that kind of incident happened today, parents on the sidelines would be pulling out their cell phones to call the league commissioner, or maybe their lawyer.

It saddens me that many kids today are so coddled. I think back to how I felt during that halftime rant. Yes, I was thirsty. But more than that, I felt humiliated. We had all let down Coach Graham, and he let us know it in a way we'd never forget. He was right. We had shown more energy at the water bucket than we had in the damn game. And getting chewed out by him meant something to us. During the second half, we went back on the field, and gave it our all.[1]

If you were fortunate to have uplifting, caring parents, neighbors, professors, and coaches you likely learned these life lessons that build resolve and self-esteem. This inner strength gives you the foundation and tenacity to commit to life-long education, to withstand and adapt to whatever job and career changes you are faced with. When you are confident in yourself, you can demonstrate the flexibility to transition and tackle new challenges and be a reliable go-to person an organization can be dependent upon. You need to exhibit intelligence and your change ability to conform to workplace innovation and transformation. Fewer US jobs going forward will be single task oriented "assembly line" type positions. Workers will be required to see and think "big picture" and continually seek to streamline processes, reinvent products, and reduce costs.

Recent surveys reveal that more than 50 percent of Americans aren't confident or are just somewhat confident their children will have better lives than they have. This is a significant shift from the wellbeing exuded by past generations. It doesn't have to be this way – mastery of the 5 Necessary Skills addressed in the following chapters can empower younger generations to create better careers for themselves and take back the promise of a better life than my (boomer) generation.

With the nature of jobs changing, job security going forward will be the knowledge of how prepared you are for the future; how financially sound you are to weather employment storms; how current your education is and its relevancy; and the skills and litheness you have mastered to create value in yourself and therefore value for an organization or your own business.

CHAPTER 2

The Ability to Recognize:
What's Going on Around You?

Recognizing what's going on around you in your job, company, and industry is the first of the 5 Necessary Skills addressed in this book, and a necessary foundation for the other four: being Proactive in your job, career and life; effectively Networking; Learning to Deal with Bad Managers and difficult coworkers; and finding and fostering Mentor Relationships. These five skills can be developed and honed to firmly put you in charge of directing your own career. To quote Jack Welsh, former CEO of GE, "Take charge of your career or someone else will." You need to be able to recognize what's going on around you and take action if you want to maintain continuous employment and upward career movement. The action may be to start a plan to find new employment, change careers or industries altogether, go back to school to gain expertise in another discipline, or change how you deal with your co-workers and managers to be better prepared for any situations that arise.

One of the most important things you can do to be prepared for any career condition or change is to be cognizant
about what is going on within your company in a micro
sense; in your division, department, direct chain of com-
mand, product suite, and coworker arena. Just as important
is the macro environment; to recognize what's going on in
your industry, your city and region, the country, and world
economy in general. Every company is vulnerable to external forces, acquisitions, mergers, innovative competitors, or
economic calamity. If a business is losing money or returning an unsatisfactory rate of return on shareholder equity,
it is ripe for some form of takeover. Another organization
may feel they can squeeze more profits from the company
or various profitable segments of the business may be spun
off from the losers. In any event, a downsizing, re-focusing
of resources, or reengineering may eventually occur for the
business to remain viable.

A company doing exceptionally well is a big "bulls-
eye" for an acquisition. A company with a great amount
of cash on hand, new technology, new processes, a large
customer database, outstanding marketing, or other lead-
ing-edge advantages over its competitors is a prime candidate to be purchased by another.

I recall a merger in the mid 1990s that was traumatic
for many New Yorkers. Chemical and Chase Manhattan
banks, both doing well on their own decided that a merger
would better prepare them for the future and competition

from the mega international banks. The result was a massive layoff of 12,000 people – most of whom didn't see it coming. There was a great deal of shock and misery around the City for months after this merger, after thousands were left unemployed from what had been good stable jobs, in profitable companies, a short time before.

Every company must move forward and grow just to maintain their market share in the new global economy, which means a constant review of their business processes, human resources, products, and marketing. What can we take away from this? It means just like the Chemical and Chase employees found out -- that just about everyone is vulnerable to losing employment, no matter what the company, their position, or industry. Certainly, belonging to a fast growing, visionary organization betters the odds for continuous employment. But even companies like Microsoft and Google have gone through periods of downsizing. The fact is that everyone should be watching for "red flags" of pending change in their workplace, at all times, for a healthy dose of reality and *positioning* yourself for the future.

The Internet has made it possible for just about anyone to find out information about his or her company or a prospective new employer. Check out press releases, competitors, and trade associations. Another way to learn of business risks was brought about by the passage of Sarbanes-Oxley Act in 2002 (and we see many more new regulations imposed following the Great Recession). The act established new accounting and reporting standards for all US publicly traded companies. It doesn't apply to privately held companies. Debate continues over the perceived benefits of Sarbanes, but supporters contend it was necessary in restoring confidence in the country's capital markets. Opponents claim it is costly, making US companies less competitive, and that regulatory requirements stifle growth and innovation. Regardless of where you stand, records are now public about business risks and can be an excellent source of information about your future prospects—either in your current job or one you are considering for a career change.

Carol Kleiman, author of *Winning the Job Game*, (someone I have respected for years)—reading her weekly columns on employment issues in the *Chicago Tribune* and as a syndicated columnist—points to some things to think about in connection with your job when danger signals emerge that your company is preparing to enter the layoff mode:

- Will you be replaced by a computer (software) program?
- Do you work in a profit center of the company, rather than so-called soft departments such as public relations or human resources?
- How many people can do your job?
- Do your managers describe your work as "essential" to the company and tell you you're "indispensable"?

- Are your responsibilities increasing or decreasing?
- Do you bring in new business?
- Are you included in new projects?[2]

Corporate downsizing shouldn't be a surprise to anyone. It is not a random decision, as the company must remain in a position to make money and needs workers to do so—it's just a matter of which ones. But most of us just aren't reading the signs of pending reductions in headcount, and think we are somehow immune.

The intent of this book is not to make anyone feel like a paranoid schizophrenic—that their job is at risk—but is instead meant to instill a healthy dose of reality that anything can happen with your employment and that a good deal of it is out of your control; but you can be **better prepared** to handle whatever occurs and protect your earning power.

Use your intelligence to watch for warning signals. In addition to those noted above, has your sales territory or number of direct reports been reduced? Are your superiors treating you differently? Are they less personable? Is your company struggling to make money? You might be perfectly okay with these changes, on the right side of rightsizing, but perhaps not. The important point here is to recognize what's going on around you and begin to heed the omen. Many times, you will begin observing changes at your organization, such as a hiring freeze, no growth in revenue in your company or the broader industry, and dwindling profit margins. You need to understand your vulnerability and channel any anxiety you feel into action—either a more stable area or department of your company, a search for a new job, or maybe even more professional education or training.

You need to identify what are you looking for in employment in both the long term as well as the short term. Perhaps in the short term you just need a job while you are going to school to complete your MBA. Or you might want to run your own business someday but need your current job to start building that stash to finance the venture.

Then there is the macro recognition of the general state of the economy, both domestic and worldwide, environmental "green" issues, your industry, competitors, new products and innovation, cheaper foreign labor, geopolitical issues, and so on. Years ago, I was invited to attend a travel industry executive conference sponsored by American Express, to hear a *futurist* speak. He noted several events that he was able to predict long before they occurred and was a very intriguing speaker. He then revealed his secret to foretelling the future to the audience. He said that he has a "war room" and simply clips out the headlines from the major newspapers, magazines, internet news services, and other media sources and tapes them to the walls. He said it is very easy to follow the trend of the various subject (headlines) and fill in what the trend tells you will be next. A past example of this would be eight years of headlines and articles about the housing bubble that would burst some day. I knew it would happen, as many people did – we just did not know the "when." Another is, we've all seen the damaging effects of the spike in energy costs, particularly the high price for oil. Thomas Friedman, in *The World is Flat*, published in 2005, clearly stated the cold, hard facts about the increasing demand for oil especially from the emerging economic giant – China. "If current trends hold, China will go from importing 7 million barrels of oil today to 14 million a day by 2012. For the world to accommodate that increase it would have to find another Saudi Arabia. That is not likely…"[3] This is China alone. We're not even talking about the other emerging behemoth India, nor the growing economies of Russia and Brazil. We're all vying for limited resources and costs will continue to escalate – and you don't have to be a seer to make that prediction. The take away – if you are involved in an energy intensive industry, have great distances to ship products, or heavy travel requirements in your company – is to be aware that something will have to *give* as you price more expensive energy into your product or service, or have to cut costs elsewhere to remain competitive.

I was involved in a leveraged buyout in which entire layers of management were given walking papers. My job was eliminated, after twelve years with the company. During that time, I had received major promotions every two years, working my way up from being a sales representative to a staff vice president. Rumors were rampant prior to the LBO about downsizing. I could see layoffs coming, and I knew I had made some enemies along the way—being the outspoken person I am. The president and chairman appreciated my candor, but the next level down wasn't overly pleased with my directness and honesty; so I knew I couldn't count on their support. I knew it could happen, so I was prepared mentally and I was well networked. There were clear signs from the people who knew I was on the list by their behavior toward me—such as not making direct eye contact with me. Or showing simulated interest in some situations I brought to their attention. Sure enough, I was among those given walking papers.

If you are observant and have good interpersonal communication with your superiors, you will have a strong idea of things to come. When you know something isn't right, it is critical that you act to get a head start on finding your next position. Management is sworn to secrecy during restructuring planning; so do not expect to get a straight answer when you ask about your position. Taking action is especially important when you are part of a massive layoff of thousands of people, because all of them will be after the few available jobs on the market.

It's all about recognizing what's going on around you and acting on the information, according to Carol Kleiman.

- Be proactive about protecting your job. When appropriate, ask how you are doing. (You need to know.)
- Have a personal strategy. Figure out where you want to go and then plan a way to get there, including your time frame.
- Be informed. Do your homework so if your department, company, or industry is in for bad times, you won't be caught by surprise.
- Add extra value to your company. Bring to the job – and use – skills not included in your job description. For instance, if you're a computer whiz, I, for one, would never fire you.
- Ask questions whenever you have them of colleagues and managers. And carefully watch everything going on around you.
- Stay competitive in your position.
- Show flexibility at all times, from accepting new assignments in a positive manner to welcoming new employees and encouraging colleagues. And even if computer programs are a challenge for you, don't resist when new ones are introduced. Be smart: Embrace new technology.
- Be part of the office grapevine or you will miss out on valuable information. Use it as a power base. But don't participate in or even listen to anything destructive about your colleagues. (Know for sure that if you do, you are next.)
- Be friendly with everyone, even people you don't like.

It's not being hypocritical: It's being smart. Avoid cliques. Avoid backstabbing and vicious office gossip.

- You don't have to be best friends, but do be respectful of your team members. You can't get anything done without them. Your performance review and salary increases depend on how productive they are. Be there for them and they will be there for you.

- Avoid office politics, which are negative, but positively form friendships and alliances that advance your career without damaging anyone else's.

- Make yourself invaluable by offering to work whenever needed, volunteering for projects (especially management's favorite ones), and brainstorming with others to reduce bottlenecks.

- Avoid office romances. They're nothing but trouble. And one thing certain about them is that they are never a secret. Everyone knows immediately.

- Keep your sense of humor; it's better to laugh than to cry—even at the office.

- Don't ever feel your job is secure for a lifetime. It isn't.[4]

When you are well informed, you are armed with and can process information to better prepare you for the future. Religiously read trade journals, the Wall Street Journal, and business magazines so you are in the know about what the economy is doing, your industry, your city, and your company. Then take action. This may be to make a job change, start looking for another career or industry to work in, or go back to school to gain expertise in another field. During difficult economic times, no one can promise you a safety net, but there is a lot you can do to ensure stability. Seriously consider a plan to change occupations to work in a field expected to see strong growth over time. (See the Chapter Eight - Where Will the New Jobs Come From?) You might want to consider a move to another part of the country where there is much more growth and stability.

The key is to use your intelligence and act on what you learn. I don't mean quit your job today and move to an electric power windmill farm in Montana – but figure out what is best for you long term and start making decisions to get there. Like saving enough money for a move to another city (if you are forced to), keeping out of debt so you can weather a period between jobs, and persist in getting educated and re-educated. If the job you have now is getting you nowhere slowly – then use it to fund your effort to start the process for a positive change – perhaps in another field or even in another part of the country. You will have to use your own intelligence and knowledge acquired by careful observation and study to be prepared for the future. As we recently found out, we can't depend on the institutions of corporate America or our government to take care of us – we have to be smart, be proactive, and take care of ourselves.

CHAPTER 3

Being Proactive

"Winners make it happen vs. losers let it happen."
Denis Waitley

Once you develop the skill to Recognize what's going on around you, how do you use all of the information assimilated? It's all about being proactive and realizing that you are ultimately responsible for your actions. There is an absolute need to Be Proactive to continuously "step up your game" to keep progressing in your career or to minimize potential disruptions and unexpected employment changes. Whether a job change is forced or on your own terms, you need positive career choices to maintain your standard of living – and the more knowledge you have the better prepared you will be to take the *bull by the horns* and to protect your earning power.

So often we are in a mindset that we are trapped in a job and therefore cruise along on autopilot, at the mercy of our employer. With relatively high unemployment numbers, it is easy to see why so many people believe they better stay put and not make any waves. But this mindset leaves you vulnerable to your employer's whims – especially if you hunker down and "just do your job." This mindset says don't question processes already in place, go with the status quo, and don't come up with new ideas or products for risk of outshining or offending your boss. But you could be setting yourself up for a headcount reduction.

One of the dumbest things you can do in a tough job market is wait for the ax to fall. Certainly, if you sense something is about to happen with your job, you are foolish not to be proactive, to get your resume updated (it should always be up-to-date) and begin a job search immediately. But what I want to convey is much deeper and long term oriented. Stephen R. Covey says it best – what Being Proactive is all about. "While the word proactivity is now fairly common in management literature, it is a word you won't find in most dictionaries. It means more than merely taking initiative. It means that as human beings, we are responsible for our own lives. Our behavior is a function of our decisions, not our conditions. We can subordinate feelings to values. We have the initiative and the responsibility to make things happen."[5]

Most employment placement companies say it now takes one month for every $10,000 of annual salary to find a new job; e.g. if you earn $100,000, it would take you ten months to find a comparable job, on average. The *Wall*

Street Journal reported, in the throws of our past recession, that most companies gave employees severance payments equal to (only) one week's pay for each year of employment. Obviously, this excluded the CEOs walking away with their millions (golden parachutes) from bailed out financial companies.

Let's use the above example of an annual salary of $100,000 and four years of employment. This leaves a shortfall of nine months salary if one were to get laid off and take the *average* time to secure a new job. Could you maintain your current lifestyle for those nine months? Do you have $90,000 in a "rainy day" savings account? Would you have to rob your 401k and deplete your retirement nest egg?

Let's face it consumerism, commercialism, or whatever you want to call it – Madison Avenue (via the Internet) has turned us all into instant gratification freaks. And employers contribute to this. Your employer wants you to look sharp and professional – unless you're locked in a bunker maintaining racks of servers. That means keeping up from a fashion standpoint – nice Brooks Brother's suits or Nordstrom's dresses – and you better have a late model European sedan to impress clients when taking them out to lunch. Not everyone has these requirements, but you get my point. You are pressured to spend what you earn and then some: To join the right club, be seen at the right places, ski in Colorado, vacation in the Caribbean and so on.

One of the best nuggets of "proactive" advice I've listened to recently is to get your financial house in order. With the uncertainties of continuous employment (recently driven home to us) we all should strive to stay out of debt and maintain a minimum of six months salary in savings at all times. Nine to twelve months is far better, especially if you have some "hefty" installment debt. By being proactive (thinking about what the future could hold) and limiting yourself to moderate house and car payments, and eliminate short term credit card and installment debt to the bare essentials, you would be in a much better position if some situation (out of your control) resulted in the loss of employment. Millions of people lost their homes in the downsizings of the early 1990s and again in the 2008-2010 period, when the greatest numbers of foreclosures occurred since the Great Depression. This, hopefully, was a sobering wake up call for all of us. Most people are not prepared for the length of time it takes to find a new job, nor for the decrease in salary they may have to accept in a new position.

In a Minneapolis-based company I was affiliated with, which was losing money for some time, there had been one round of lay-offs and rumors were rampant about additional lay-offs. Senior management was in continuous closed-door sessions. Employees, at all levels, were scared to death about losing their jobs. I knew some of the "frantic" people and asked what they were doing about the situation. "Worrying a lot," was the response. Very few had put together resumes, contacted employment agencies, or actively started looking for jobs. I guess there is some deep-seated belief in most peoples' subconscious that gives them false hope that "it can't happen to them." Well, guess what? Several hundred additional workers were laid-off and most were in a state of shock, "how could this happen to me and with no advance warning." In fact, the warning signs were all around them.

Religiously study trade journals, blogs, business reviews, and follow the stock market to know what is going on in your industry and related businesses. This will give you all of the clues you need about the long-term condition of the industry and stability of the companies comprising it, not to mention your own organization.

Networking is also invaluable to learn about the viability of your field and to meet potential employers – to open doors, if need be. (The entire next chapter is devoted to networking.) You never know who your next employer may be. Clients, customers, or business associates potentially hold the keys to your next job. Join as many applicable trade organizations, such as the Direct Marketing Association, the American Society of Travel Agents, the American Institute of Architects, etc., as you can handle. Be active in them and meet your counterparts from other organizations. Attend all of the industry functions that you can, and get to know individuals from a variety of firms and you will acquire a great deal of knowledge about your industry.

In your own company always accept the opportunity to serve on committees, CRM teams, reengineering task forces, planning committees, or any other group selected by management or co-workers. This can provide valuable recognition of your contributions to the organization and position you as a reliable, go-to person. It can also give you tremendous insight into what's going on in the company -- on subjects like new product lines, new company directions, rightsizing, plant closings, process changes, etc. which could very likely affect your job. Whenever additional training or educational seminars are offered be the first to volunteer. It will put you a step ahead of others who chose to sit on the sidelines.

In a recent Harris Poll, over one-half of respondents indicated "very likely" and "somewhat likely" to the statement that "You will have to have formal retraining in new job skills to maintain your standard of living." Radical changes within many organizations are needed for companies and their employees to remain competitive in the global economy. This doesn't just involve market assumptions but what products you develop, how you operate, new competitors, environmental concerns, worldwide operations, and even the planning process itself. These revisions require new, creative thinking and a continuous updating of skills—change ability is key. Working on an advanced degree or a certificate in a field or discipline, such as Six Sigma, can only enhance your ability to progress in your company and remain a valued employee, as well as increase your paycheck. A four year college degree still earns 89% more than less-educated peers.

There was a period in the late 1980s and early 1990s in which it was more difficult for MBAs to find jobs to justify their additional education. But they came back in demand with a vengeance in the late 1990s and early 2000s – with the Internet creating huge demands for workers with advanced technology degrees. Now, as we emerge from a period of slow growth, an advance degree doesn't assure you a great job but it increases your odds of getting one. If you already have practical experience in a field, an MBA can only enhance your value to a company, therefore, your promote-ability in the long-term. Keep a broad based focus is the only caution. The changing job market requires flexibility. However, there are countless articles in the media today which suggest the only people being hired, in this tough job market, are those with the "exact" set of skills the organization is looking for. Recruiters only want to see resumes that perfectly match the specific job requirements. Companies use software to scan resumes for keywords that perfectly match the position to be filled. Interviews are only scheduled with candidates with recent, highly relevant experience.

Conversely, we read that workers with skill sets, which were too specific, were the ones being cut as many companies downsized in this past recession. This makes some sense. If you have fewer workers or managers to do the job, they are going to have to take on expanded roles - not only completing their previous assigned responsibilities but perhaps manage unrelated departments or jobs as well. But wouldn't it also make sense for lean companies just starting to expand their workforces out of the depths of recession, to hire well-rounded individuals who have the capability to do a specific job and the wherewithal to assist in other areas?

That's the dilemma for job seekers today. Do I pigeon-hole myself into a position vis-à-vis my resume and the interviews and get pitted against others with those exact skills? Or do I let my broader experience shine through and risk being labeled with less than the concentrated practice they are searching for? The experts say that college graduates should keep a broad based focus since the changing job market requires flexibility. Workers who already have gained practical experience in a field may be encouraged to add additional education – such as a finance degree to their repertoire, to enhance their value to an organization.

The reality is that smart, progressive companies – the ones we all aspire to work for – are going to opt for the person with more than just the expertise to perform the job at hand. You probably want to pass on the opportunity if the company is so compartmentalized that they don't want you to think out of the box they are attempting to squeeze you in to. The balancing act is to get through the screening of your resume and the gauntlet of preliminary interviews by "playing the game" with your "exact fit" for the job. Once you have an audience with senior management you can showcase your well-honed transferable skills—as well as the ability to do the posted job. It will require nimbleness, but that's what today's job market is about. If the key decision-maker doesn't feel confident of the additional value you will bring to the organization, you may not get the position. But you now have a margin of control over your own destiny, by having all of your cards on the table.

We may learn something from the Generation Xers about being more dependent on ourselves. Unlike my baby-boomer generation that had the delusion that we could take the future pretty much for granted, the Xers are more apt to think long term. The Xers I've worked with, in several start-ups, never expected to work in one job forever, which instilled an avoidance of dependency and has made them generally more flexible—with loyalty centered within themselves as opposed to any organization. I think they have done a much better job at investing their own resources and nurturing diversity and adaptability than us boomers. This will help them in today's job market and hasten their success; most likely defined as personal life and career success—than the boomers' career focus.

We all are free to make choices in most situations, whether it's to join a health club, buy a new BMW, smoke cigarettes, quit your job, work longer hours, save for an emergency, or continue working for an abusive, narcissistic boss. You don't have to take into account what others think of you and simply follow their lead. If you find yourself in a bad work situation, you should proactively plan on making a change – on your terms, not theirs. The challenge of being proactive is complex – especially if you are not certain what you want to do with your career or life in the long term. That is why so many people get caught up doing the same old thing, in the same old way – going nowhere slowly – or just follow the crowd regardless of potential outcomes. It may be that you are not taking time to follow the trail to the logical endpoint. "Man I'd sure like to have a new BMW M3 – yes, they are very expensive but my friends will love cruising around with me." You may even justify it in your own mind even though you can't afford it – your current car is just fine and, oh by the way, you hate your job and its going nowhere – but I'll somehow be able to make the payments. You need to take charge and look "long-term" and create the sustainable lifestyle you ultimately desire.

Proactively use your intelligence to your advantage to understand the possibilities of what can occur with your employment. Be prepared, both psychologically and financially, for any changes that materialize. Always keep your resume updated. What matters most is making the decision to start consciously directing your own life instead of being pushed along by external forces. There is always going to be the unexpected, but you can be better prepared for it by using your brain and being proactive.

CHAPTER 4

Networking Effectively

"You give before your get."
Napolean Hill

One of the essential skills you need to master to find a job or get a promotion (market yourself), sell a product, and get projects completed in today's complex business environment is networking. Wikipedia defines networking as the act of meeting people in a business or social context. But it is what you do when you meet people, how you follow-up and remain connected, which are of utmost importance.

Networking is also one of the most common misused buzzwords of the past decade and there are many misconceptions of what effective networking is all about. An article recently appeared in Yahoo! HotJobs, in which the author's singular advice on networking was "use social networks to, well, network." This major revelation of hers amounts is no advice at all. Many people (that author included) and the media frequently confuse networking with social media "tools" (Web sites like Twitter, FaceBook, MySpace, LinkedIn, FriendFeed, etc.). These are just that, tools to facilitate networking, but have little to do with the art of effective networking.

Tom Hopkins, author and one of the top sales guru's of our time, writes, "When people use networking, they are taking advantage of a basic law – the Law of Reciprocity. That law basically says, if I do something good for you, you will feel obligated to do something good for me."[6] So whether you do something for someone via telephone, LinkedIn, at a conference, in church, or your office – it's the act, not the medium you use, that makes it true networking. And it's really fairly simple, you have to extend yourself (give) before you can expect to (get) in return.

Networking is a very underdeveloped skill with many people. It will open doors to a multitude of opportunities when taken to a higher degree. In fact, it is critical for each of us, whether managers, employees, or leaders of any sort, because it will support and maintain you in the best of times, and be your lifeboat in the worst of times. You can learn all sorts of information about an organization or individual, without prying or being overbearing, once you develop a little skill and tact. It can become one of your most important avenues to learn about a new employment opportunity or discover more about an industry, company, or key players within an organization. "My recommendation is always to make sure you're building and nurturing a network before you ever need one."[7]

Some people say the ability to network is a natural gift—one they just can't perform. While seemingly difficult, even intimidating at first, once you back away from self-imposed pressure and view networking as just chatting with people – something no one really has a problem with – it won't be stressful. The experts say almost anyone can learn how to exchange information with another, or among a group of individuals, in a friendly, helpful manner and then follow up to maintain contact and familiarity. Some common myths people have about their capability to network:

- It's difficult for me to introduce myself to strangers. This all depends on the setting. There is usually some common interest, such as your kids, if you are talking to other parents at a youth basketball game; a local construction project, if you are at a chamber of commerce meeting; the last speaker, if you are attending a trade conference; or a "topic for discussion" on a Tweetchat. Better yet, get an acquaintance to introduce you to someone you want to meet either online or in person. It is important to always have a plan of what you are looking to accomplish when an introduction occurs. Have a 30 second "elevator" conversation prepared about you and your background – so you don't come across like a deer in the headlights when asked a question. Even if you are in a career transition (since a great deal of our identity is tied to our jobs) be prepared with what skills you have mastered and your interests for the future. It's a good idea to have some personal business cards printed up if you are not representing a company – for contact information. How about those Red Sox? There is always some common interest.

- I don't know very many people. When you look back at previous jobs, your current employment, alumni from schools you've attended, your church, trade associations, other parents from your children's activities, extended families, local events and charities you are involved in, and social networking Web sites you know more people than your realize. And the Internet has made it possible (and relatively easy) to re-connect and stay connected with more people than imaginable a few years back. I was recently reacquainted with dozens of hometown friends from decades ago and keep connected with hundreds of former co-workers and business associates with very little effort on my part. Tweetchats are great to connect with others with a common interest, such as recruiters and jobseekers. (More details and the best of these follow later in this chapter.)

- I find it difficult to "work the room" when I'm attending an event. Have a plan of what you want to accomplish when you're going to a potential networking venue—conference, trade show, reception, seminar, or Tweetchat. Just about all functions have a list of attendees available on their Web site or as a handout when you register. (And in the case of Tweetchat, many publish a list of topics to discuss to help you get prepared for their rapid pace.) Take a look and determine who you would like to meet and this will give you some direction. You can even ask at the registration table if they are seen so and so, and perhaps someone can point them out. Remember that first impressions are lasting impressions. Your appearance is very important (to be noticed) and can be a good start to a conversation. "That is a beautiful evening gown." "First time at this conference?" Limit your drinks, or consider nonalcoholic beverages so that you will appear alert, intelligent, and most importantly, sincere. Don't be pushy and force your way into a conversation, but wait politely for a pause to introduce yourself. Most important is to listen empathetically to the answer when you ask a question. After a polite conversation, if this person is not someone you wanted to meet, move on. Exchange contact information if it is appropriate. End with a solid handshake and "It was nice to meet you." If you have been involved in an Internet chat, follow up with a personal email.

- I don't want to sound self-promoting. This is a healthy hesitation to have because it is not about selling yourself. In fact, that will ruin a good networking opportunity. It's all about finding some common ground with the other person, connecting with them and forging a relationship. There is an ugly stigma associated with networking brought about by people simply out to hock their own product or service – so it is critical that you practice the art of listening, with subtle inquiries about the other person. You need to be engaging with him or her acknowledging what they are telling you. There will come a point when a "connection" occurs and you will find a natural opening for sharing information you believe is pertinent about yourself. You need to be respectful of what they are telling you and, as Napoleon Hill suggests you've "got to give before you get." Offer your assistance to the other party – perhaps an introduction to someone or name of a company or business contact who could assist them – and open the door for future discussions. Do not ask for a job, act desperate or for an introduction to someone. They must offer this or other advice first – and that will only happen after you have extended yourself and your network to them. Only then offer to exchange business cards or contact information. Don't discount anyone you meet. It may be that the person you view as not an important contact may be able to introduce you to someone you are trying to meet. This has happened to me on several occasions. While the person I met was not the right contact in an organization—they were able to *open the door* to the person I needed to see.

Two of the most important points of effective networking are to thank the other person for connecting you, making an introduction, or any other assistance they provide. (Nothing will nurture the relationship better than a solid, appreciative thank you for their help – via email, telephone, or better yet a handwritten note.) Secondly, to follow through with what you say you are going to do. Whether it is to email your contact information to them after the meeting, to pass along information about an opportunity, or contact someone they suggested (and let them know about it). It is important to carry business cards and a pen in any potential networking situation or to immediately update your Blackberry or iPhone. When a conversation has ended, very inconspicuously make a few notes capturing the information you learned about this person for follow-up purposes. This is necessary for the important follow-up, which will keep your network fused together.

Networking within your company is just as crucial to your career as external contact. It is important in that it gives you visibility to other employees and managers, and different departments of your company. It can open doors for a promotion or transfer to a "better fit" position for you, or out from under a lousy boss. You should volunteer for every possible committee, company sports team, holiday party planning group, charity events, training seminars, etc. that you are capable of doing. It will not only give you valuable exposure throughout your company but also keep you better informed about your workplace and all opportunities within.

Networking is necessary, in today's multifaceted business environment, to be able to complete projects and assignments you are given. With all of the downsizing that has occurred, each remaining worker was forced to take on more responsibility – with, or without, any additional training (or money). Many workers lack all of the knowledge they need to complete many of the added assignments, as jobs have become more complex—or they just involve more work than one person can handle. Star performers turn to others to get help, to their networks to increase their productivity. You need to start by recognizing what you don't know and then who has that knowledge. You need to find and develop relationships with those people and always be on the lookout for co-workers to add to your network. And realize that networking is a give (before) you take barter system. If you expect people to help you, you have to establish that you have something you can offer them. You may have to help out a lot of people before you get anything in return.

There are many settings for meeting others who may be in a position to provide you with insight about a business opportunity, where you are prospecting for information about a company or potential employment. These are receptions, conferences, trade shows, social networking Web sites, conventions, on an airplane, a sales call, church, your daughter's dance recital, extended family, an alumni association gathering, or just about anywhere people come together. A networking relationship can evolve from keeping in contact with former sorority sisters, business associates, professional associations, other departments within your company, or classmates.

There is effective networking and ineffective, lousy, "user" contact some believe is networking. We've all witnessed the loud, obnoxious, insincere individual who butts into a conversation, then doesn't listen and is constantly looking over to the next group for someone more important to meet. Or there is the person who only calls or e-mails when she needs something and conversations are all about her. Networking is not just contacting someone on a social networking site and assuming because you know someone they know, they will recommend you for a job or give you access to a business opportunity. I rate the most significant networking attribute to be sincerity; whether it is an online introduction or just sticking out your hand and saying, "Hello, my name is…" Genuinely show interest, exhibit empathetic listening and good interpersonal communication will be established – potentially leading to a solid networking relationship. Through casual conversation, e-mail, or IM you will find out names, companies, positions, etc., while giving out the same information about yourself and your network. You must be subtle and listen intently, in order to be successful. Again, offer your assistance always before you ask for any from them!

Several social networking Web sites make connecting with others relatively easy. I mentioned Tweetchats previously, which are communities formed on Twitter. The best I have found connecting both recruiters and jobseekers was founded by Margo Rose, a HR and social media professional and evangelist for jobseekers. Her goal is simple: "to use social media for social good. I want to change the world for the better. The #HFChat and #HireFriday Community helps all candidates move their career forward. Whether you are looking for a job, or just thinking about making a change in the future, the HireFriday Community is here to serve you. Each of you has the potential of being a true community steward leader. The beautiful thing about the HireFriday and HFChat communities is that each of you has a sense of belonging, and the joy of leading a purpose driven life. We do this by networking, and being of service to one another. Again, it is all about building community, a community that is rich in resources, filled with support, and provides real-life business development." Her Web site is http://hrmargo. com and she participates on LinkedIn and Facebook as well – definitely worth checking out.

The business social media site used by many professionals, which brings together traditional face-to-face networking with more up-to-date methods, is LinkedIn. Launched in 2003, LindedIn is now one of the largest professional sites and adds about 1 million new users every two weeks, according to their spokesperson Kay Luo.

The following is a blog used with permission from Guy Kawasaki, author of *The Art of the Start*, on "Ten Ways to Use LinkedIn to Find a Job."

Searching for a job can suck if you constrain yourself to the typical tools such as online jobs boards, trade publications, CraigsList, and networking with only your close friends. In these kinds of times, you need to use all the weapons that you can, and one that many people don't—or at least don't use to the fullest extent, is LinkedIn.

LinkedIn has over sixty million members in over 140 industries. Most of them are adults, employed, and not looking to post something on your Wall or date you. Executives from all the Fortune 500 companies are on LinkedIn. Most have disclosed what they do, where they work now, and where they've worked in the past. Talk about a target-rich environment, and the service is free. Guy Kawasaki offers a blog of the Ten Ways to Use LinkedIn to Find a Job through networking.

Here are ten tips to help use LinkedIn to find a job. If you know someone who's looking for a job, forward him or her these tips along with an invitation to connect on LinkedIn. Before trying these tips, make sure you've filled out your profile and added at least twenty connections.

1. Get the word out. Tell your network that you're looking for a new position because a job search these days requires the "law of big numbers" There is no stigma that you're looking right now, so the more people who know you're looking, the more likely you'll find a job. Recently, LinkedIn added "status updates" which you can use to let your network know about your newly emancipated status.

2. Get LinkedIn recommendations from your colleagues. A strong recommendation from your manager highlights your strengths and shows that you were a valued employee. This is especially helpful if you were recently laid off, and there is no better time to ask for this than when your manager is feeling bad because she laid you off. If you were a manager yourself, recommendations from your employees can also highlight leadership qualities.

3. Find out where people with your backgrounds are working. Find companies that employ people like you by doing an advanced search for people in your area who have your skills. For example, if you're a web developer in Seattle, search profiles

in your zip code using keywords with your skills (for example, JavaScript, XHTML, Ruby on Rails) to see which companies employ people like you.

4. Find out where people at a company came from. LinkedIn "Company Profiles" show the career path of people before they began work there. This is very useful data to figure out what a company is looking for in new hires. For example, Microsoft employees worked at Hewlett-Packard and Oracle.

5. Find out where people from a company go next. LinkedIn's "Company Profiles" also tell you where people go after leaving the company. You can use this to track where people go after leaving your company as well as employees of other companies in your sector. (You could make the case that this feature also enables to figure out which companies to avoid, but I digress.)

6. Check if a company is still hiring. Company pages on LinkedIn include a section called "New Hires" that lists people who have recently joined the company. If you have real chutzpah, you can ask these new hires how they got their new job. At the very least you can examine their backgrounds to surmise what made them attractive

to the new employer.

7. Get to the hiring manager. LinkedIn's job search engine allows you to search for any kind of job you want. However, when you view the results, pay close attention to the ones that you're no more than two degrees away from. This means that you know someone who knows the person that posted the job—it can't get much better than that. (Power tip: two degrees is about the limit for getting to hiring managers. I never help friends of friends of friends.) Another way to find companies that you have ties to is by looking at the "Companies in Your Network" section on LinkedIn's Job Search page.

8. Get to the right HR person. The best case is getting to the hiring manager via someone who knows him, but if that isn't possible you can still use LinkedIn to find someone inside the company to walk your resume to the hiring manager or HR department. When someone receives a resume from a coworker even if she doesn't know the coworker, she almost always pays attention to it.

9. Find out the secret job requirements. Job listings rarely spell out entirely or exactly what a hiring

manager is seeking. Find a connection at the company who can get the inside scoop on what really matters for the job. You can do this by searching for the company name; the results will show you who in your network connects you to the company. If you don't have an inside connection, look at profiles of the people who work at the company to get an idea of their backgrounds and important skills.

10. Find startups to join. Maybe this recession is God telling you it's time to try a startup. But great startups are hard to find. Play around with LinkedIn's advanced search engine using "start-up" or "stealth" in the keyword or company field. You can also narrow by industry (for example, startups in the Web 2.0, wireless, or biotech sectors). If large companies can't offer "job security," open up your search to include startups.

11. Build your network before you need it. As a last tip, no matter how the economy or your career is doing, having a strong network is a good form of job security. Don't wait until times are tough to nurture your network. The key to networking (or "schmoozing"), however, is filled with counter-intuitiveness. First, it's not who you know—it's who knows of you. Second, Great schmoozers

are not thinking, "What can this person do for me?" To the contrary, they are thinking, "What can I do for this person?" For more on schmoozing, read "The Art of Schmoozing."

Here are two more ways I can help you in your job search. First, for an aggregation of hundreds of newly posted jobs, check out Jobs.alltop. Second, to really stay on top of what's the latest news about LinkedIn, go to Linkedin.alltop; this will turn you into a true LinkedIn power user. Just remember me when you're rich and famous![8]

Networking requires a plan and a conscious decision that you want to network effectively. As mentioned, the first thing you want to do if you are attending a trade show or conference is to review the list of attendees. You can usually find it online before you arrive or pick up a copy as you register. You can set priorities of whom you want to meet and what you want to accomplish.

Just as important as the first meeting is your follow-up—the effort to maintain contact. There are several excellent database management software programs available today, like Salesforce.com, ACT, iPhone apps or even Apple's Mac calendar, that can remind you of important dates or reasons to call or email. When you meet someone you want to get to know better, drop him or her a note or e-mail stating that it was nice to meet him or her. Keep it short and sweet but suggest a future meeting, telephone call, or lunch to prepare them for the next contact (but it will be strictly up to them whether to accept this overture of not). If you run across an article that you think would be of interest, drop them an email with the article—it will show your professionalism and thoughtfulness. Don't try to accomplish too much—save additional questions or comments for subsequent meetings. And always offer your assistance to them first, before anything is requested.

Some "old school" so-called networking experts suggest that you send everyone you meet birthday and holiday cards. Unless you know the person well, I find this practice to be obnoxious. Birthdays are personal to most people. I don't need someone I met at a cocktail reception six months ago wishing me happy birthday. To me, this is not sincere: what do they really want from me?

A good excuse to e-mail or write to someone is when you see a noteworthy new advertisement or product introduction for their company. Attach the ad or email the page and comment on its effectiveness or ask about the new product.

Networking takes a little courage. Remember the old adage, "Nothing ventured, nothing gained." I was trying to line up appointments with key travel industry executives in Australia and not having much success. One of my business associates, from Australia, used to be a director at the transit authority in Melbourne. I asked for his assistance, and he got me an appointment with an Australian Senator and the Minister of Tourism for the state of Victoria. Using that appointment as a base for the importance of the services we were selling, I readily obtained appointments with all of the companies I was targeting. (Name dropping worked in our favor in that situation.)

Not one of the six jobs I have held during my adult life was discovered in traditional employment search methods—they were all basically found by networking. While working for a franchise of a major corporation, I had the opportunity to handle a transaction for the district manager of the parent corporation. As a result of friendly conversation and asking the right questions, I found out he was in town to hire a sales representative. I applied for and got the job. Twelve years later, after an LBO and lay-off from that company, I made contact with some former executives who now ran a competing company. I was hired to run a new division of that company, after a couple of interviews. A client I was calling on, to sell our market-ing services, offered me the next position in a different but related industry I had wanted work in for years. The job after that was obtained by keeping in contact with a former business associate and learning of a position avail-able right where my wife and I were hoping to relocate. I then was hired to run the business-to-business sales and marketing organization, of an Internet company, after lis-tening to a sales pitch by their director of sales. He ended up reporting to me.

As I mentioned, a networking plan is necessary — it's

important to have a plan for anything you want to accomplish. It should be complete with the How, What, Where, and Why – what tactics will you employ and what are your goals. Set up whatever format works best for you, but I believe the plan should be in three parts: internal, external, and social networks.

- Internal Plan (within your company) – You need a plan for a network within your organization just as with the outside world, to get noticed for promotions and to keep a pulse on how your company is doing – it's long term viability (and yours). Talk to co-workers in other departments. Determine where you might have a better "fit" and who the best managers are—ones who will help guide your career.

- External Professional Plan – these are the organizations, trade and professional groups you should belong to for long-term career growth and development. Join as many trade and professional associations as your schedule will permit. Develop strong relations with colleagues in these organizations. They may be able to help target a career search down the road (if need be). Former company co-workers may be valuable in the future to introduce new opportunities to you – and you to them. Alumni associations – former classmates, as they spread their wings and end up in different industries, in various parts of the country (or world), you will want them in your network.

- Online/Social Networks - I strongly believe, just as you cannot physically be in two or three places at the same time, you cannot effectively keep up with too many social networks. I would limit it to two or three that you can really keep up-to-date and pay attention to. There is cross-over with the Internal and External plans here because you will most likely use online social network sites to keep in touch with your former classmates and professional organizations. But keep the plans distinct and separate with a reference for the "medium" you will use to keep in touch. Important: You never know who will be checking out your various social media or professional sites so keep everything above board. It's good to show you know how to relax – but before you post anything, think of a potential employer scrutinizing the post – because they will.

Always, always, keep in mind that when you meet someone, from an organization you are interested in, the last thing you want to do is "get in their face" and ask for a job or introduction to someone. They must take the lead to get you to the right person or give you pertinent information, to help you sell a product or find a new position. Never forget to acknowledge assistance by a solid thank you – preferably in writing, and offering your services to that individual.

Networking works—when done effectively. With a little practice and chutzpah, you will have a great advantage over those who think they are networking because they have a Twitter account, or sit back in the shadows and don't pursue the opportunities available from all the people they come in contact with.

CHAPTER 5

Dealing With Bad Managers

How many times have you heard a friend or colleague say "I hate my boss – she is horrible and making my life miserable?" When you hear it again and again, it is difficult to be sympathetic when absolutely nothing is being done to change the situation. There are many variations but it's the same sad story—almost as if they are completely helpless and have no responsibility for his or her own life and livelihood. If you are proactive, you are not going to sit back and endure a horrible workplace experience. Eleanor Roosevelt said it best, "No one can hurt you without your consent."

Too often we are on autopilot and accept what a company dishes out or the questionable behavior of a mediocre manager. Especially in today's tough job market you will hear "jobs are scarce and I can't afford to risk making a change." But these are usually the same people who complain a lot, and shoulder stress, without taking action even in prosperous times.

While your immediate boss may give you the biggest headache (at present), we have witnessed the damage done to our nation's economy, the near collapse of our financial and mortgage markets, trillions of dollars of savings and millions of jobs lost by the actions of a handful of top executives in several of the largest (too big to fail) financial and mortgage institutions. (You can add a lack of oversight by our federal government to the list of culprits.) Between Angelo Mozilo, of Countrywide, Richard Fuld, of Lehman Brothers, Martin Sullivan, of AIG, Stan O'Neal, of Merrill Lynch, and James Cayne, of Bear Stearns, millions of jobs were decimated as their failed companies crippled the economy. This disastrous group of CEOs make the last decade list of narcissist corporate leaders, Jeff Skilling, of Enron, Bernard Ebbers, of Worldcom, and Al Dunlop, of Scott Paper, appear not much more dangerous than playground bullies – even considering the damage they caused. The lesson to learn is that top executives can have a devastating impact – not only on your job and company – but tens of thousands of others in related businesses. We always need to be aware of the actions of the top executives of our places of employment, as well as direct managers, and how they will impact our livelihoods.

Carol Dweck, Ph.D., in her book *Mindset*, describes the CEO wanting to be seen as perfect—often called the "CEO disease." She says CEOs have a choice: "Should they confront their shortcomings or create a world where they have none?" She describes many brilliant CEOs who chose the latter and got caught up believing their own press releases—that they could do no wrong.

One of the symptoms of CEO disease these top managers possess, as well as wanting to appear perfect, is they surround themselves with people who have the same ideas, attitudes, actions, and, at times, appearance. You'll find a short CEO encircled by "shorter" men and women, or a fast-paced person by other "hyper" types, or an autocratic leader by other repressive types. It can seriously stifle the creativity and progression of an organization if the leader hears no criticism or dissent from his or her lieutenants. Warren Bennis, author and leadership guru, coined the term "Doppleganger effect" to describe this. It's the phenomenon where some autocratic leaders, narcissist CEOs, or just plain insecure managers encircle themselves with others who reflect their own philosophies and management styles. Warren Bennis goes on to say:

Of course, this is perfectly human and understandable -- up to a point. The huge size of such organizations and the enormous overload burdening every top leader make it impossible for him to verify all his own information, analyze all of his own problems, or always decide who should or should not have his ear or time. Since he must rely for much of this upon his key assistants, he would not feel comfortable in so close and vital a relationship with men who were not at least of kindred minds and of compatible enough personalities.

This means, of course, that the leader is likely to see only that highly selective information, or those carefully screened people that his key assistants decide he should see. In a very critical situation, he may discover only too late that he has acted on information that was inadequate or inaccurate, or that he has been shielded from 'troublesome' visitors who had something to tell him he should have known, or protected from some problem that should have been his primary concern.[9]

Professor Bennis points out why a leader of a company finds himself surrounded by people only agreeable with him. He also describes the dangers to the organization he is charged with running. How can you make the "right" decision when you don't have all the available facts, because someone spoon-fed you information *they* decided you should hear? If you don't have associates or subordinates who provide both sides of a problem, they perform a disservice to you and the organization. This will eventually catch up with the leader and, consequently, those shielding him or her from pertinent information.

Lee Iacocca felt threatened by new ideas and innovation by his lieutenants at Chrysler, that they would get credit instead of him and diminish his self-proclaimed godliness. He only wanted "yes" men and women around who showered him with praise. He fired many rising young stars because of his paranoia that they would out-shine him. (I'm sure they were distraught at the time, but it was probably for the best to get out from underneath his reign.) This got so severe that he became a petty tyrant and was finally given walking papers by the board of directors, as the company lost its competitiveness that Iacocca had worked so hard to create just years before.

Is there a right way to "challenge" the boss, or is agreeing with her the only way to stay on her good side? Most yes men and yes-women are fairly easy to identify in many organizations. They may not be the gutless wonders and suck-ups we think they are. Depending on your career goals, it may be helpful to agree with every lame idea or thought your boss comes up with. That is, if you are only worried about keeping your job in tough economic times. But if you plan on getting promoted in an organization, it's not wise to be branded with a yes-person title. The management team won't perceive you as someone who can creatively solve problems. Yes-people may perform set tasks okay but are not known for their creativity and challenge of existing processes.

The senior executives I have encountered in my career who have been the most vocal about not wanting yes-men around are the very ones who surround themselves with the biggest suck-ups. They seem to be the most insecure, or afraid of losing their authority, and lash out at anyone who offers a differing opinion—hence, no one around them will dare challenge a single word. Believe me, when one of these tyrants "jumps down someone's throat" for voicing their opinion, new ideas and creativity suffer tremendously.

I recall a marketing board meeting I was participating in, where the Senior VP brought up a thought and went around the room for opinions. Everyone agreed with him except for me. When it was my turn, I told him why it didn't make good business sense. He tore my head off, complete with expletives deleted. Then he asked everyone to think about it in more detail while he left the boardroom to take a call. As soon as he was gone, everyone agreed with me that it was a harebrained idea, but that they wouldn't challenge him. When he returned, he concurred with me that it was a stupid idea that would never work. The other board members remained in this Senior VP's organization. I gradually lost his favor (he wanted to be surrounded by yes men and women), but left the company on my own terms and timing - determined not to play his game.

In another organization, the CEO was defending a pricing decision that the company had recently made to lead the industry out of a price war. We were in the number five market share position and had failed miserably two years before to lead the industry in a pricing increase. He mentioned we were giving a choice to the intermediary sellers of our service, and this would give us a competitive advantage. In fact, we were not giving the sellers of two thirds of our business a choice, because we could only display one price in their computer systems. I mentioned this, and I came armed with screen shots to back up what I said. He went off on a rampage and said I didn't know what I was talking about, and why hadn't anyone else brought this up to him. (Because his direct reports knew exactly how he would react to questions regarding his decision, and they didn't want to incur his wrath—that's why.) This "attempted" pricing change was a dismal failure, with none of our competitors matching. Some inside estimates of the losses caused by this pricing mistake were in the $30 million range. I made the judgment call to leave this organization based on this CEO's close-mindedness. I personally cannot stand by silently when a serious error in decision-making is going to cost an organization millions of dollars. Not that you are going to agree with every decision made nor will you typically have all of the background information that the top executive has. But when I have the information and the narcissism of the executive keeps him or her from listening or requesting more facts before they make a decision, I don't want to work long-term for that organization.

One thing I have learned is not to openly offer a dissenting opinion in a group, especially to a strong-willed person, but to catch him or her alone after the meeting. They appreciate the input much more, at that time, than having to defend their idea before the whole group. However, in any setting, a truly successful, open-minded executive will absorb all feedback and consider it as being valuable to his or her decision-making process.

Small groups, whose members have highly developed interpersonal skills and are challenged to speak out by someone they perceive who has the power to make things happen, are the opposite setting of a boss surrounded by yes-people. Many companies set up these types of project teams, which are meant to foster openness and cut through layers of bureaucracy. Top executives should cultivate these groups whenever possible. And you should try to become a member of such groups, if you get the opportunity. This will allow you to voice your opinions without any fear of challenging the boss and to be recognized by other team members.

Yes-men and yes-women can succeed, but in the long run, those who challenge the ideas of their bosses will get farther ahead ultimately, although perhaps at a different company. Challenge with finesse and tact, such as in the question form, "Have you considered this other point of view?" Or, "Let me play the devil's advocate for a moment." And know your boss. If he or she cannot deal with conflict, you had better not deliver any if you want to remain in good graces. His limited scope of information will eventually catch up with him.

Just about all managers and supervisors in this country got their positions because they performed their previous jobs well. There is the age old "You are a good salesperson, so we're going to make you the sales manager." (Typically, a big mistake, because they require radically different skill sets.) Or you were a shining star in the customer service center, so we're making you the supervisor. But many companies don't offer adequate training on skills for managing other people. How you are supposed to know the skills and qualities to become an effective supervisor of others? By luck or chance? Or perhaps you worked for a good supervisor and observed what they did right (or wrong that damaged the moral of the workers) and learned how to (better) manage a team. When companies tighten their belts, there is usually even less investment in training. So literally thousands of untrained supervisors and managers are operating in the *dark*. This can have devastating effects on the job performance and satisfaction of their subordinates. These companies typically end up with high turnover rates (compounding their problems), lousy productivity, and poor customer satisfaction. It's a snowball effect—loss of unhappy customers, budget cutbacks, less profit for training programs, even poorer employee performance— and still more customers going to competitors. The impact on these companies can be measured in billions of dollars of lost sales opportunities.

What are the warning signs that your direct manager is out to get you or just doesn't have a clue about supervisory skills—perhaps getting promoted for being a good worker (the Peter Principle from above)?

1. She doesn't support you when things go wrong or gives you an assignment, but doesn't follow up.
2. He acts paranoid and needs to know everything—in a very micro- managing way.
3. She doesn't know how to plan or prioritize tasks.
4. If it's not his idea, it isn't any good.
5. She makes conclusions, with very few facts to back it up.
6. He is always teasing or making sarcastic jokes.

If you have concluded that your manager is not out to make your life miserable but is definitely lacking in managerial skills and will limit your growth potential in the company, you should develop a plan. First, find someone you can trust for a reality check. If they agree you are caught up in a negative environment, you might want to start with a "positive" confrontation with your boss. Perhaps you can come to an understanding about how you can both work better together. If this backfires into a "negative" session, with no meeting of the minds, and the issues are serious enough to damage your productivity, set up a meeting with your human resources department to discuss the issues. They may have heard these same complaints from others, and this will push them to take action. You should also be learning how to perfect your own supervisory skills by experiencing the "how not to do it" first hand. You may also want to put feelers out within the company to see what positions are available in other departments or even outside the company—especially if things are really rocky between you and your manager and you don't get a sense they will improve.

Stephen R. Covey adds a valuable point: "Don't let yourself become a victim of your boss's weaknesses."[10] If you are trapped behind someone close-minded and unwilling to change, maybe the time is ripe to leave on your own accord. Remember, "you can't soar like an eagle when you are surrounded by (or report to) turkeys!"

Some recent research conducted by Florida State University, found that roughly 54 million American workers -- 37 percent -- have been bullied at work. Employees in these destructive settings suffer from tension, stress, and even depression. This certainly leads to a lack of job security – either you are being forced out – or you know you must make a change. Sarah Burgard, a sociologist at the University of Michigan, in an article published by LiveScience.com says "In fact, chronic job insecurity was a stronger predictor of poor health than either smoking or hypertension in one of the groups we studied." She goes on to say that "Based on how participants rated their own physical and mental health, we found that people who were persistently concerned about losing their jobs reported significantly worse overall health in both studies and were more depressed in one of the studies than those who had actually lost and regained their jobs recently."[11]

There are generally about seven types of managers most people categorize under the lousy boss heading: 1) never available and does not communicate or give direction, 2) always critical, denies worker contributions, big ego built up at subordinates' expense [the bully], 3) no backbone, will not stand up for team, and will not make decisions, 4) multiple bosses, with little or no coordination of workload, 5) overachievers who set unrealistic expectations, 6) the micromanager, and 7) creates an unhealthy environment by repressive behavior and harassment.

How do we deal with one of these manager types and maintain our sanity, let alone survive and prosper in our company? Some thoughts:

1. How do you deal with the boss who doesn't communicate with you and expects you to read their mind, and is not available for direction? This is probably one of the common complaints about bosses. Fortunately, e-mail and cell phones make people a great deal more accessible than they were in the past. Though people have to read e-mail and respond to make it work! With all of the reduction of staffs that recently went on, your boss may just have too many responsibilities (or direct reports) to handle any effectively. Whether this is the case or not, you have to set up a meeting with her to detail your concerns. You should document the times you did not know or understand something, perhaps not putting you and your boss in the best light. If she is just overloaded, you might suggest

ways in which you can help her. Part of the problem may also be that you go to her piecemeal, as opposed to noting many questions you have and going after all the answers you need in one session. So she doesn't feel barraged with your communications, try to set up one regular meeting or call each week, at the same time—to take care of all but emergencies. Always be succinct, with just the facts, to be respectful of her time. If all this doesn't work, you will have to go to others in the company for help—but tread cautiously so your boss is not offended (by your end run). Always keep documentation of what was communicated to you and what you did based on the request.

2. Then there is the boss with a big ego, usually built up at his workers' expense, who denies credit for any contribution. This boss is a typically a bully. Big egos are a problem, as I've addressed in dealing with CEOs at the beginning of this chapter. You are not going to change the narcissism of this individual. You can try to live with it and feed it to a certain extent—by continuing to work hard and produce quality output. Eventually, your contributions will become known, no matter how much credit this individual tries to claim. This is tough though. You will have to bite your lip and wait to be noticed. One way around this is to volunteer

for projects, committees, CRM control teams, and company events. This will get you exposure to other departments and managers within the company, and recognition will eventually come your way. If working for this person becomes too painful, make a plan to get out from underneath him or her. This may be applying for other positions in the company or leaving the company altogether. If it is truly an unhealthy work environment with public belittlement, up to and including employee harassment, see your human resources department. Again, document what is going on around you. See harassment in #7.

3. The boss, with no backbone and who doesn't stand up for her own team, can eventually self-destruct. Because the only way for her to pat herself on the back (legitimately) is by giving her team kudos for a job well done. But it can be problematic (perhaps it can take years). You should start by delicately asking for her support and defining areas or situations in which you need it. You and your fellow team members will have to stand up for yourselves if your boss will not support you. This may be done by copying other departments or her boss on e-mails and memos to subtlety let others know what is going on. As in #2 above, volunteer for any and all projects out of the department, so others in the

company will see the results you and your team produce. If decisions aren't being made—stifling the output of the department—eventually it will catch up with her. But in the mean time, you are going to have to go to her superior for help, especially when an important decision or missing a deadline is at stake.

4. How do you handle the situation, in the newest work environment, where you report to two, three, or more people— as is the case in many companies dividing work by projects, teams, or work groups? This can be a challenging and rewarding environment that you should make the most of. But there are only so many hours in a day—and hopefully you have a life outside the company. You need to document what is expected of you, what you are working on at all times, and keep detailed estimates of the time it will take to complete various tasks. If there is a conflict, someone trumping someone else's priority, you must get the two parties together and have them settle what is to be completed first. This doesn't have to be, and should not be, confrontational. Just a detailed statement of the tasks, time requirements, and a decision. In other situations, if multiple bosses are pulling in different directions, as with every other situation, document what is going on. It may take your multiple

bosses' boss to settle it.

5. Another tough situation to be in is if your boss is an "overachiever" and has unrealistic expectations of you and your team members. This probably could be combined with #4 above—as it frequently happens in the fast-paced organizations built around projects and work teams. You could most likely label 4 out of 5 entrepreneurs in start-ups in this boss category. The overachievers believe everybody ought to live and breathe the company just as they do. But a big difference is that they stand to gain the most if the endeavor is successful. In these organizations, you need to work smart and as hard as you can to get ahead. Make it known that you can work late hours part of the time, but not all of the time. If you have children, school, or other commitments—just say NO to the extra hours. But teamwork does require that you go the extra mile at times; so put forth the extra effort when you can. Odds are that your boss will recognize you for your contribution and you will move upward in the organization. But until you establish what you can and cannot do, the unrealistic expectations may continue. Make sure your performance and output is the best it can be, and this boss will think long and hard before ever replacing you.

6. Working for the micromanager is another extreme. It is very hard to learn and grow in an organization if you report to one of these control freaks. It makes sense, when you are new in a position, to have someone look over your shoulder to ensure you have caught on to the job and are not making mistakes—but enough is enough. When they continually worry about the smallest detail and offer unwanted and unnecessary advice, even when you have mastered the job, you must ask for a cease and desist! A good defense can be a good offense. Try giving them details of everything you do—report on all activity—until they yell "uncle!" They will either realize they have been overbearing or that you know every fine point of your new job, and back off. You still may have to confront him or her, but go armed with documentation that you know what you are doing and how stultifying it is not to be able to do your job.

7. The repressive boss who creates a hostile work environment may be the greatest challenge you will have to deal with. Fortunately, there are federal and state laws against harassment in its various forms. These are addressed next in this chapter.

There are a lot of good, caring managers in the workplace and some lousy ones. This chapter began with the problems and challenges you may incur with executives with "CEO disease" and then down to your direct manager; but there are also out-and-out illegal and discriminatory practices that you must be aware of and prepared to deal with. Most of us know that discrimination in hiring and firing, promotions, assignments, compensation, testing, training, or use of facilities based on race, color, religion, sex, national origin, disability, or age is against the law. But, also any employment decision or opportunity (once employed), based on stereotypes or assumptions about the abilities, traits, or performance of individuals of a certain sex, race, age, religion, national origin, ethnic group, or an individual with a disability, is illegal. Any type of harassment or retaliation against someone filing a charge of discrimination is against the law. Again, most of this is pretty cut and dry, but some areas of discrimination are not.

One observed time and time again in the workplace is sexual harassment. We laugh at the sitcom *Office*, but as we know, some of these seemingly outlandish situations actually occur in the real world. Sexual harassment includes practices ranging from direct requests for sexual favors to workplace conditions that create a hostile environment for persons of either gender, including same-sex harassment. Favoritism and cronyism can often be a by-product of sexual harassment and can damage the moral of an entire department or organization if left unchecked.

Also keep in mind that pregnancy based discrimination— meaning pregnancy, childbirth, and related medical conditions—must be treated in the same way as other temporary illnesses or conditions.

If you find yourself in a discriminatory environment or one of harassment by a manager, it typically only gets worse and worse. You will have to, most likely, endure a painful period of time, as you finally determine you must take action, and do so. If you are caught up in one of these situations, contact your human resources department right away. If they do not take you seriously, immediately investigating the complaint, then contact the Equal Employment Opportunity Commission (EEOC) in your area—using their Web site is the easiest way to begin the process.

You may experience the misery of working for an awful manager or a company with a greedy, self-serving CEO during periods of your career. Not only will you have tension at work, but it can leave you stressed and anxious at home – even make you physically ill, as recent studies have shown. If the company is a good fit for you and you like the overall environment—with the exception of your boss—you might want to seek out a position in another department or division, as mentioned previously. It is important to keep flexible. A woman I know was a manager in her company's HR department but detested her director and the poor service she gave their customers—the company's employees. She loved the company and didn't want to quit, so she applied for a training director position and got it. She's now as happy as she can be in her new job and has very little interaction with her old boss.

When you can just tolerate your manager, who may have reached his or her level of incompetence, one thing you can do is get someone to mentor you—to help you navigate the potential "landmines" within your company. The benefits of mentors will be addressed in the next chapter.

If you are truly unhappy with your job, don't delay— start taking action. List the jobs or industries that interest you, and then consider your special talents and skills. Next, make a determination of the career choices that mesh well with your strengths. Don't rush this project. Make sure to talk to relatives, neighbors, associates, and friends about pluses and minuses of their jobs. (But don't whine about yours – nobody wants to hear it; just make informational inquiries.) Attend professional networking events and job fairs. Network on LinkedIn and Tweetchat career discussions, to learn more about people and available jobs. Consider going back to school for an advanced degree or a specialist field. Become aware of the possibilities in the market place, where you won't feel stuck in a job working for a narcissist, with concern not for his employees but only himself. It is really a shame that companies (and their boards) don't realize when they have these managers in their ranks—looking after their own interests instead of the company's until it's too late, such as in the case of the latest Wall Street and financial institutions meltdown.

You will have to make the decision of staying in a

particular position or in a company with awful management. If you are learning something and progressing in the career, you might want to remain in your position, at least for a time. But be prepared for your next gig—life is too short to be at the whim and mercy of a rotten boss. Suck up when you need to. But keep the decision to leave on your timeframe—not his or hers—and get prepared for a change.

CHAPTER 6

Find and Foster Mentor Relationships

Just what exactly is a mentor and why are they important for your career? A mentor is "a coach, a friend, someone to give advice," in the classic dictionary definition.

A mentor can be a career game-changer in the complex bureaucracy of large corporations. How can a fresh recruit out of college, or any new employee for that matter, possibly navigate her way through the corporate bureaucracy of a 10,000 employee company with subsidiaries, divisions, departments, purchasing, marketing, and even branch locations? Or even a small business, which must have a banking relationship, an accountant, a taxman, an advertising or marketing company contract, suppliers, customers, and others. It's a stretch to think that someone should walk into a position—and be able to figure out the organizational communications, structure, and culture— to become a solid contributor, in fairly short order. So ideally a mentor is someone with more experience in your company, or another organization, who can share their experiences about how to get things done and communicate effectively within the business.

In the past, mentoring was all about senior managers, usually men, tutoring bright young "clones" of themselves. Women were virtually excluded from the mentoring process just like they were treated like second-class citizens with their pay scale vis-à-vis men's. Now, one-half of US workers are females (and over 50% in Canada) for the first time in history. In 1960, only 30% of the workforce was female—and men dominated the management ranks—with the ratio of women's median pay to men's around 60%. Even today, it has only risen to 80% (largely because of the bloated salaries of CEOs and top executive ranks still held by males). All you have to do is look around corporate meetings and business flights and it is easy to discern that females will, in short order, make up half of all management ranks. Mentoring programs have to be brought into the 21st century to prepare our female and minority leaders of tomorrow (and equal pay must be enacted).

Young women are hungry for advice on how to succeed, with the rapid growth of females in the white-collar workforce, but women who have already risen in the corporate ranks don't always have the extra time to mentor the next generation. The "old school" of mentoring needs an overhaul to be inclusive of all employees.

The way mentoring used to work, a senior executive

would anoint a younger version of himself as his protégé, the operative assumption: Mentoring was all about chemistry between two people who had a lot in common. It was also about connections—the mentor, who was several rungs higher up the ladder, could steer the lower man toward career-enhancing projects or plum assignments.

Fast-forward to the present. Women have poured into the new world of work, and they've found they aren't welcome in the old boys' club of mentoring. They can't rely on men to pick female protégés. They can't depend on being able to socialize in the old style—on the golf course or over a cigar—to form personal bonds. So women have changed the rules. They've invented formal practices where none existed before, making mentoring more organized and focused.[12]

Many companies admit it has been easier for aspiring young men to get mentored by senior men than it is for talented young women or minorities, since white males continue to hold the senior positions in most organizations. But companies have realized, now that women are earning more college and advanced degrees than men, that for their own self-interest they must see that females and minorities are given the same tutoring and encouragement. Because they will soon be occupying an equal number of corner offices and executive positions. Progressive companies have set up formal mentoring programs realizing their futures depend upon it.

My experience has been that (mentoring) relationships, which have grown *naturally* over time, perhaps because someone has worked for me or I have worked for them and we have developed mutual trust and a certain bond, have contributed a great deal to each party's growth. Yet, while mentoring has typically been about someone taking a junior employee under his or her wing, where certain chemistry existed, it is important to correct the imbalance of the past male dominated mentoring by establishing formal programs.

My wife works for a large national company, and she helped launch her company's formal mentoring program, where employees can select a mentor from a list of more seasoned volunteers. She continually mentors 3 to 4 people and is mentored herself by a more senior level executive. One of her greatest challenges is managing expectations. She finds the new workforce, the millennials (Generation Y), many times have somewhat difficult to accommodate expectations about their employer's role in providing a balanced life for them—giving them job flexibility in hours—for their personal life-balancing needs. Many even have a sense of entitlement—that the company owes them this. Carol Kleiman echoes this balance requirement. "Other groups are tuned in to the promise of a balanced life: A majority of undergraduates name it as their top career goal; single people say they have a right to it, too; Generation Y, the 29 million Americans born from 1981 and on, are extremely vocal about making the demands of their work lives fit the demands of their personal lives. And deserve our admiration for sticking to their standards of what makes life worth living."[13]

While businesses know that millennials are their future workforce, many have the same concerns about expectations—and mentoring can help to condition them for the "real" world. Yes, you want to give them (the group in general) credit for putting the (important) priorities of a personal life ahead of a company's, but you must have employment to enjoy a personal life; so they are intertwined. Most companies have a problem with letting employees shape their jobs to fit their lives versus the other way around. Millennials were raised with so much admiration that they now seem to require a great deal of attention and positive reinforcement from their supervisors on a (almost) daily basis. They have great expectations of what companies must do for them, but are they going to exhibit any loyalty in return? This is where more seasoned mentors can play an important role in helping this generation see the two sides of the scale and perhaps moderate their expectations.

Judith Lindenberger, President of The Lindenberger Group, discusses how the experienced and younger workers can help each other for the overall betterment of the organization:

Younger employees routinely tell us of their disen-chantment with their companies as they describe the onerous demands (and opportunities) placed on them by managers who may have confidence in their abili-ties, but lack the time or skills to help them succeed. Faced with frustration and afraid that they will fail, many of these younger employees tell us that they are planning to move on and look for a more supportive business environment. In fact, the average 30 - 44 year old has had up to ten different positions.

Most businesses could use their more experienced baby boomers, who have deep knowledge, impres-sive networks, and broad-based business experience, to buffer younger employees against frustration, focus on their career paths, and find places to acquire the skills-based knowledge necessary to succeed.

To be effective, mentoring needs to be done strategi-cally and creatively. Here are some benefits and guide-lines from our experience.

Make mentoring a strategic business imperative. Studies show that there is a positive correlation be-tween a positive mentoring experience and an increase in productivity, employee retention and job satisfac-tion. Effective mentoring, however, is a tremendous time commitment on the part of the employee and the mentor. It will not work unless the company strategically acknowledges the value of mentoring by adjusting the mentor's other business responsibilities. Modeling from the top also works well. If your head of operations at a particular location is a mentor, it sends a powerful message to employees about the value placed on mentoring, and also the focus on people as the most important part of your business.

One senior VP at a financial services firm regularly mentors five or six people... unless he feels that his skills set does not match the mentee's goals. Then he will recruit a more appropriate mentor for that individual. He sets stretch goals for his mentees and then provides them with tools and strategies to meet those goals. He often encourages them or selects them to present in front of senior management using their new skills.

Provide new perspectives. Encourage older workers to stop defining themselves in terms of their job titles and start reflecting on skills they have built, and knowledge that they have amassed. Today, jobs are about more than just upward mobility. Mentors can share their vision and career histories so that younger employees understand what they can learn through lateral career moves and on the job experience.

Share information. Mentoring can help boomers quickly learn about other levels within the organization. Says one mentor at a Fortune 1000 company, "As a leader, it has helped me to see the obstacles we inadvertently put in people's development." Mentoring can also help mature employees learn from and understand other generations. For instance, younger employees can help baby boomers with technical skills or provide marketing insights about a new generation of buyers.

Build skills. Mature workers benefit from being mentors by having the chance to learn more about and practice listening and coaching – skills which require maturity, confidence and experience to fully employ.

Reduce generational conflict. The most frequently reported generational conflicts are differing expectations regarding work hours, certain behaviors at work (e.g., use of cell phones), and acceptable dress. Another common issue is feeling that co-workers from other generations do not respect one another. Organizations can reduce generational friction with effective communication, team building, mentoring and recognizing the efforts of all workers.

Enable knowledge transfer. As baby boomers retire, they take with them volumes of experience and information. Good working relationships between older and younger generations are critical in ensuring that this institutional knowledge is not lost as mature workers retire. The greater the mix of generations in an organization's workforce, the more important knowledge transfer becomes and the more powerful intergenerational synergy can be.

For example, younger employees often push back on managers, questioning the corporate rules and regulations. Typical questions may include, "Why do we have to come to work at 9 am?" or "If I come in late, why can't I make up the time?" Mentors can often manage, explain and process this information differently and at times more effectively than managers.

During the 1980s and 1990s many companies laid off significant numbers of employees. Now organizations are faced with large numbers of employees getting ready to retire and the need to bring onboard younger workers and quickly move them up to supervisory and managerial positions. Younger managers may come to their new positions with little or no business-related experience and have trouble building their own credibility and integrating and respecting the knowledge and talent of mature subordinates. Mentors can help these new managers develop business-related understanding and strategize about using the talents of more experienced employees.

In our experience, we have seen baby boomers who are reluctant to mentor younger employees because they are afraid that once they share their knowledge, they will become extraneous and lose their jobs. In fact, in today's fast-paced business environment, it is the SME's (subject matter experts) who can capably and articulately share what they know who are the most valuable to their organizations. Here are some tips for encouraging baby boomers to pass on organizational knowledge.

Reward, don't punish, mature employees for mentoring. To entice baby boomers to become mentors, organizations should reward and recognize them for their contributions. Talk up mentoring in meetings, in speeches, in newsletters, in performance appraisal discussions and include mentoring in corporate awards programs. And, most important, don't replace mature mentors with their mentees before they retire or mentors will quickly conclude that being a mentor is a very bad idea.

Ask mature employees about someone who enabled them to succeed. In one study of people who had experienced effective mentoring, half of them said the mentoring experience "changed my life."

Those are powerful words. It is equally powerful to know that you were the person who changed someone else's life.

Share mentoring results. Study after study in which mentors and mentees are asked how satisfied they are with the relationship report that the mentors are more satisfied. It just feels good to help someone else. Says one mentor; "It has been rewarding to be able to help people at critical stages of their career by helping them analyze where they are in their careers. Mentoring gets people in the right groove for long term career success."

Encourage mentors to pass on their life lessons. A key component of domestic saving in the United States in future decades will be the personal saving rate. That rate will depend on a number of factors, especially the behavior of baby boomers. As a mentee commented, "My mentor has helped me think about the future and gave me advice like start saving for your retirement today. The two percent on the personal side is really powerful."

Continue mentoring past retirement. The trait most attributed to baby boomers is the willingness to give maximum effort. Baby boomers are also rated as highly results-driven, very likely to retain what they learn; and low on their need for supervision. Many baby boomers plan to work at least part-time past the traditional retirement age. These characteristics show baby boomers to be eager workers who may be well suited to be brought back as consultants and mentors after their retirement.

Mentoring is a process that is compatible with baby boomers' values and work style. Mentoring involves being collegial, talking, sharing (not telling), and developing solutions together. It is also optimistic, which is typical of most baby boomers' outlook on the world. We've found that when generations work together in strategic, business-related activities such as mentoring, everyone benefits. The mentee builds new business knowledge, and the mentor often gets re energized and reengaged in business opportunities. We find unique satisfaction in nurturing these synergistic relationships.[14]

Contact Judith Lindenberger, President, The Lindenberger Group www.lindenbergergroup.com for more information about mentoring and careers in general.

A mentor program can provide real, tangible results to a company and give an enormous boost to the mentee's career and long-term development. It can help you avoid the corporate "landmines" which the mentor has learned to navigate around. While some mentoring relationships form organically, you need to set up a deliberate plan of attack to find a mentor—the right mentor to jump-start your career (especially) if your company does not have a formal program. What should someone look for in a mentor – what qualities make the ideal mentor? All successful business people are not necessarily effective mentors – certain individuals are just more effective in developing others. I like the Winston Churchill quote, "We make a living by what we get, we make a life by what we give." Some people just have more patience, the ability to listen, genuine interest in other people, and the willingness and desire to counsel others. Some are just too busy in their own worlds to lend a helping hand – and mentoring cannot be a rushed activity. Research suggests that the best mentoring relationships are those in which protégés chose their mentors themselves – someone who you admire and trust – which are two of the most important mentor qualities. Someone who is patient and has accomplished many of the things you are aspiring to do. If you want assistance to advance in your career it is helpful to have a mentor a couple of levels of management above you – who has been in your position and understands the organization, its challenges and mission. But mentors can be from any level – even a peer – to bounce around ideas and challenges. Pick someone with a good reputation for helping others (if you can discern this). Those from Generation

Y, who are tech savvy, make great technology mentors to more senior executives.

Before you seek a mentor for your career (or life for that matter) you need to honestly do a self-evaluation and consider where you are at that point in time. What are your strengths and weaknesses? What are the greatest challenges you face in your position and with people in your organization? What tests you each time you are given a task to complete? Getting others to contribute? Finding answers to questions? Or other tasks and time constraints pulling you in different directions? You have to assess your needs and what kind of personality you have to know the best fit for interacting with another. Do you have the necessary education or training—or is that holding you back? What do you want to be doing in 3 years? Only when you answer these questions can you begin to understand what type of mentor can best assist you. If you want to progress in your career from here to there – you've got to know the starting point.

Typically the best mentor is someone right in front of you. Someone you have gone to for assistance, who you respect and trust, who has gone out of his or her way to help and genuinely shows interest in you. It could be someone in your company, a minister, a family friend, a professional colleague, a college professor, a coach, a former boss, or even a racquetball partner, who you respect and regularly get advice from. Again, you need to know what type of help you (generally) are looking for and simply ask if the person would consider becoming your mentor. Leave them an easy out though – you don't want someone to agree but then not put the energy behind it to make it work. Suggest that you know they have a great deal on their plates but wonder if they could make the time to meet with you periodically as a mentor. This way if it is not right for them they can gracefully decline and you can remain friends (most people will be flattered that you asked). Certainly, experience in your field or the overall workings of a similar company increase the value of a mentor in most cases.

For entrepreneurs or small business managers there is an organization called SCORE – acronym for Service Corp Of Retired Business Executives. They volunteer their time to coach small businesses and their operators. Most major cities have SCORE organizations.

Keep in mind a mentor does not have to be someone in a position senior to yours – it could be a trusted colleague to bounce ideas and questions off of as a reality check before you embark down a particular path. Networking with professional associations can help you find a mentor in your field. Numerous women's organizations have sprung up over the years like the Society of Women in Engineering, the Culinary Institute of America for men and women, and others – which have networking events and formal mentoring introductions.

Another business owner you become acquainted with at a Chamber of Commerce event might be a big help, from both their own failures and successes perspective. They could help you from going down a dead end path from their experience.

What are the primary ingredients of a mentor – mentee relationship? It's the same for the protégé as for the mentor – respect and trust. If you are told about a past incident at a company to help you avoid a similar pitfall – the mentor must know you will keep it in confidence. You must be proactive in the relationship and exhibit a great deal of energy and enthusiasm to keep the relationship fresh and moving forward. This positive attitude will directly influence the time and commitment a mentor will provide to his or her protégé.

Listen, listen, and listen some more and you will learn a wealth of information. Acknowledge corrective criticism but don't react. You need this impartial advice and this may be the only place you will get it. Ask for advice on how to overcome the issue. You must be flexible with time to meet another's schedule—perhaps coffee before work or an occasional lunch away from the office. Sincerely thank your mentor for her time and how much she means to you professionally.

Some of the topics suggested for discussions between mentors and mentees, from a local company with a formal mentor program:

- Don't bring your manager problems, bring her solutions. What does that mean? Can you give

examples of times when this is done and times
when it is almost impossible to do it?

- Peer one day – boss the next. This is possibly the
most difficult transition someone is asked to make
in their professional career and here is no training class or guide to use. What are the pitfalls and
things to watch out for?

- Do you advance your career by being a good
specialist or generalist? What are the specialties
and generalities respected and rewarded in your
company?

- Our company hires from within whenever possible, but must also bring in talented people from
the outside. What makes some people excel and
some people bomb?

There are couple notes of caution. One is not to bring
complaints about your boss or specific problems with other departments to your mentor. She is not there to replace
the human resources department and this will quickly sour
the tone of the session. Also, never develop a false sense
of security that your mentor will come to the rescue if
your job is in danger – either from a performance standpoint or a reduction in staff. I have observed this on a few
occasions, and have personal experience, where a mentor
was a senior executive (one even the president of a company), and they could not (or would not) step forward to
intercede. As the definition says, they are a coach or friend

there to give advice, not someone to run interference.

In spite of the need for treading carefully, it can be an enormous benefit to you (and your career) to acquire the knowledge and wisdom a good mentor can provide. There are a great many caring people in most companies who want to look after and mentor employees with less tenure. Learning from these individuals is invaluable to navigate corporate cultures and organizational communications. Develop realistic expectations and respect for your managers and fellow workers in order to earn their respect. Always keep an open mind about who might be a good mentor—as mentioned previously; diversity in a mentor can provide a unique perspective on you and your needs you otherwise might not uncover.

The best way to keep your relationship continuing with your mentor(s) is to sincerely thank them for the time they spend with you and the advice they provide. When you make them feel important to your career development and how much they mean to you professionally, they will likely continue the mentoring for as long as is desired.

CHAPTER 7

The 5 Skills in Practice: Maintaining Your Self-Worth and Taking Charge of Your Career

The 5 skills can be instrumental in maintaining continuous employment. There are no guarantees in life, but you can stack the deck in your favor by developing these skills. More important than any job, is maintaining your self-worth. If you develop and practice these five proficiencies, you will be a step ahead of the game. Not only will you feel more secure about your future and how you make a living, but you will exhibit confidence and be more productive. Let's review the 5 skills and the upward spiral of your career that can be set in motion by their adoption:

The **ability to recognize** what's going on around you gives you a better understanding of your industry, products, competitors, and the economy in general. This will make you a more well-rounded, knowledgeable, and valuable employee and give you the insight to better position your company in its marketplace, and gather intelligence about your future. Being **proactive** helps in all of your business dealings, whether it's getting a report done on time, thinking of your customers' needs before they do, or implementing a beneficial, new process before your boss asks you to. And positioning yourself for "change" if need be. Learning to **deal with lousy managers** or self-centered company officers can give you an advantage over your coworkers. If it becomes unbearable, only you will know it's time to move on to another organization. But if you are still learning and progressing in the company, you may want to manage the situation a little longer until timing is right to make a move. A **mentor** can assist you to navigate the corporate "minefields" and position you to move ahead in your organization. The more information you have at your disposal, the better equipped you are to handle situations that arise in your company. **Networking** with industry colleagues, old college friends, church groups, or any others can only increase your knowledge of the job market and enhance your marketability. You are taking care of yourself, your career, and building your self-esteem all at the same time.

Many people wait for something to happen or someone to take care of them. But the people who end up with the good jobs are the proactive ones who are solutions to problems, not problems themselves, who seize the initiative to do whatever is necessary, consistent with correct principles, to get the job done.

Proactive people are still influenced by external stimuli, whether physical, social, or psychological. But their response to the stimuli, conscious or unconscious, is a value-based choice or response.

As Eleanor Roosevelt observed, "No one can hurt you without your consent."[15]

If we are to maintain our self-worth in the face of adversity, these quotes from *The 7 Habits of Highly Effective People* are critical. When you know that you control your own destiny, and recognize what is going on around you, you cannot blame others for what happens. If a company goes out of business, or downsizes and lays you off, you would certainly feel distress and nervousness about the future. But if you knew that you had worked hard each day and contributed all of your talent, then you could walk away with your head held high—knowing that you had done your best for the company.

Your integrity is what you are all about. It's your self-worth—your soundness and honesty. If you are not contributing great value to the company or the tasks that make up your job, you must ask for more to do or that a process be streamlined—even if there is a risk of eliminating a significant part of our job. It is far better to continually look for better ways to do things than for someone else (manager or consultant) to uncover tasks that are unnecessary (that are currently being performed).

Companies can also help with employee confidence and increase productivity as a by-product. After all, self-image is not ours alone—outside stimuli are significant contributors. A lousy manager or top executive can wreck havoc with employee confidence. There is strong evidence that low self-esteem directly relates to low employee performance and conversely high self-esteem produces the highest performance. Companies and their management who provide an environment and recognition programs to encourage worker self-esteem will be the winning organizations going forward. When you are being rewarded for coming up with new, helpful products and ideas, as well as being flexible in what you do for your company, they win—and you win, most likely progressing up the management ranks.

For your personal success it is necessary for you to develop proficiency in your job, which will reinforce the notion of a win/win situation where workers are treated well by employers.

1. How well you communicate determines how quickly you will move ahead.

2. Being able to handle your own financial matters, including your individual negotiations for salary and benefits, is essential to advancing your career.

3. You will be judged by your familiarity with your company's human resources policies and your ability to meet its expectations of you as an employee.

4. Your knowledge of information technology, continually updated, is a basic tool for your personal and professional requirements for success in today's technological society.

5. Having finely honed interpersonal skills means you can get along well with management, staff, and particularly your team members.

6. Leadership skills on a personal level mean stepping in when necessary and offering suggestions or even taking charge unofficially—until the day when you actually do take charge.

7. Management means taking care of your career in a proactive and well- informed way.

8. Marketing means aggressively (but not too aggressively) promoting and selling yourself to the company and your colleagues to show you're a serious player with serious ambition.

9. Getting your arms around process management means you understand firsthand what is involved in getting your next promotion or your next choice assignment—and working to make sure you're considered for both.

10. Project management means creating for yourself and working by yourself on projects that,

when completed, will enhance your value to the company. An example: taking responsibility for supplying information, with your manager's approval, to your company's Web site about your department's achievements.

11. Purchasing management, as it relates to your career, is knowing and making sure you have the tools you need to be successful in your present job, including electronic equipment, support stall, training, and continuing education.

12. Sales/customer service means being knowledgeable about the market you are serving and understanding the needs of the consumers you are trying to sell to. In addition, on a personal level, it means being aware of the needs of your supervisors and doing whatever you can to meet those needs.

13. Strategic management is exactly that: Develop a strategy to manage your career—and follow it. Strategically.[16]

Gurcharan Das, the Indian CEO for Proctor and Gamble, has been quoted on numerous occasions about what it is like to contribute all of your effort to the job at hand by being totally immersed in what you are doing. He says, "It is absorbedness—total contentment in work so engrossing that you don't even know that you are working. It may be working early morning hours without even realizing the time going by because you are so content in what you are doing."

Most of us don't have the luxury of working for an employer who is deeply concerned about our happiness and contentment. Most businesses have somewhat pleasant environments, but virtually no one goes out of their way to make sure that you're happy.

You have to take responsibility for creating the work environment you wish to establish with your work team. When you (and they) are content and confident, the whole team is more productive. You don't mind putting in whatever hours or effort it takes to get a project done and make sure it is done correctly. When you have a good mentor, you have additional insight into what's going on in the company and what you can do more effectively. To get ahead in business, and stay ahead in your job, requires learning to deal with various coworkers and their personality differences—not just showing up for the job. You should try to get some insight into the habits and work manners of those coworkers you are in regular contact with. You have to keep your head and use common sense when a coworker "loses it" and gets abusive. Exit stage left—as diplomatically as possible. You don't want to enter the fray. Whatever the subject of distress was, it can be dealt with better at a later time with cooler heads, when a professional atmosphere returns.

Learning how people like to interact with you is critical in communications with them: are they more verbal, or do they like written messages? Do they like "just the facts" or the complete, detailed report? Are they more communicative in the morning or afternoon? It is up to you to determine this and position yourself—by being observant of your coworkers—to get the most out of relationships. By cultivating these associations, it will make your time at work much more pleasurable and trouble-free. Make sure you gain exposure outside of your work group by volunteering for committees, sports teams, or the holiday party planning group, as I've suggested previously. This will help you form bonds with others in the company and can potentially be helpful as your name comes up for promotions.

Employees must be proactive and learn to adapt and upgrade their skills in order to succeed and move up in the business world of today. Education must be continuous—throughout our careers—to stay ahead of the game. It is estimated by the U.S. Dept. of Labor that three quarters of all workers currently employed will need to be retrained for new jobs that are created daily by new technology. Companies also know their workforces have to be trained to remain cutting-edge to keep their organizations competitive, though during tough economic times training budgets can take a hit.

Carol Kleiman offers this on the significance of training programs:

"Training is so important that, according to the

American Society for Training and Development, companies have been spending an estimated $65 billion a year on employee training—at least that was the size of their budget before the current economic turndown. My point is that the need for training doesn't disappear in a recession; in fact, it accelerates, because it is vital for companies to get the most out of the employees that remain on staff. That's why all the large employers devote entire departments to worker training. Some even have their own 'colleges'—actual campuses at which their workers study and learn. Others invite accredited institutions to come in and teach various courses, including foreign languages, and to offer degree programs, including bachelor's and master's degrees. Smart employers know that training and being up-to-date keep them competitive. Radisson Hotels & Resorts, based in Minneapolis, announced in 2002—after the recession began and after the terrorist attacks—that it was instituting "training enhancements" for its corporate and hotel employees to access training and education both in person and online. And why did Radisson, which has more than 430 locations in 60 countries, decide to do this in the face of hard times for the hospitality industry? 'We want to help our brand become best in class,' said Jay Witzel, president and chief operating officer.

And the classroom is the best place to do that.

Still, it is up to you to research, direct and make provisions for your own continuing education program."[17]

Your corporate "survival" plan revolves around work ethics. It is the realism that you must believe that you are not owed a job—that you have to earn it each day. You must respect your work group, managers, and supervisors and show that you are a reliable team player. Excellence must be a commitment—that will show you are ready for more responsibilities and (therefore) salary. And you cannot point the finger at others when you make a mistake or have work problems. These are solid work ethics and are not aimed only at the younger workers but apply equally to all workers and management.

Michael Hammer and Steven Stanton noted what they felt were traditional company values in their book *The Reengineering Revolution* (which are still applicable today). They go on to say how these values must change in order for employees to adapt to the latest management direction:

The values required for successful reengineering turn out to be exactly the opposite of the traditional ones we described.

1. It's not keeping the boss happy, it's keeping the customer happy.
2. It's not keeping a low profile and moving, it's getting things done and creating value.
3. If a problem lands on your desk, don't dump it on someone else's.

4. You must regard other people in your organization, not as enemies, or competitors, but as allies and teammates. Your future depends not on their failure, but on your own success today. You can expect help from them tomorrow. In other words, reengineering requires a transformation of the basic values that have shaped people's behaviors in large organizations for many years.[18]

The management teams of organizations have an immense responsibility to play in restructured companies to assist employees by helping them adapt to the changes and latest direction. Hammer and Stanton go on to add management's role:

The very first step is to ensure the desired values are designed into your processes. If you tell people you care about customers, yet nobody ever has the chance to interact with them, your words will at best be hot air, and worst, a symptom of hypocrisy. If you declare speed to be a competitive advantage, then make damn sure you design your processes to be fast. If you have a goal of flexibility and innovation, then the ways in which people work must be structured to accommodate variation. If you proclaim change, be sure you can handle it. An order fulfillment process locked into a fixed mode of operation speaks louder than any talk about flexibility and change.

Senior executives must walk the walk, not just talk the talk.[19]

The real message in today's business world is that employees need to learn to take care of themselves, thus creating a feeling of security and a sense of self-worth. This will make them much more responsive to the customer, both internally and externally. Give everything you've got to make your team work effectively together to create value, which is the message of *Open Book Management: The Coming Business Revolution*.

Even traditionalists—if there are any left—will recognize the buzzwords. Total quality management! Teams! Empowerment! Reengineering! The old top-down, chain-of-command style of management is out; today's boss is supposed to walk around, involve the troops, and encourage participation. Gone, too, is the notion that employees are no more than tiny cogs in a machine. Workers are now supposed to take on big responsibilities – to solve problems, cut costs, and reduce defects. The language of business reflects the new ideas. Trendy companies don't have employees, they have associates. They don't have managers, they have coaches.

Quality efforts for example, often improve quality. They don't always improve the business. At Varian

Associates Inc., a maker of scientific equipment, employees so obsessed with quality-related measures that they quit returning customers' phone calls. All of the quality-based charts went up and to the right, a Varian vice-president confesses. But everything else went down.

Teamwork and empowerment programs have their success stories -- so long as you catch them before they fade away.

Open-book management, by contrast, teaches the want-to. Instead of telling employees how to cut defects, it asks them to boost profits -- and lets them help figure out how. Instead of giving them a reengineered job, it turns them into businesspeople. They experience the challenge -- and the sheer fun and excitement -- of matching wits with the marketplace, toting up the score, and sharing in the proceeds.[20]

In my youth my father used to quote "if not by me, by whom? If not now, when?" Which meant you're not going to go play baseball with friends until you completed whatever chores he had assigned. This message obviously means a great deal more to me now than it did back then. To survive in business, you've got to be proactive and take the bull by the horns to make things happen. In business today, there is no room for "I thought that so-and-so was going to do the task." Or, "Let's wait; that report isn't due until next week." By tackling major projects head on, without procrastination, there will be more thought put behind the effort, and it should result in a more thorough and better organized end product. You cannot get the same quality when you rush to complete something at the last minute, let alone the unhealthy stress level you bring upon yourself.

There seem to be some misconceptions about Generation-Xers. The big differences between baby boomers and gen-Xers will most likely leave the Xers better prepared for long-term survival in the new workplace. They have now observed three deep recessionary periods where their parents (or friends of parents, relatives, neighbors, etc.) got downsized out of jobs; therefore, they expect less of corporate America. Consequently, they are much more dependent on themselves, and take much less for granted, than us boomers. Somewhat of a shock to me was some fairly recent research done that found Xers twice as likely as boomers to agree to the statement "money is the only meaningful measure of success." Conventional wisdom suggested that they were not as likely to be thinking of material wealth as boomers at the same age, with more concern about their next "adventure" than their job. But to avoid dependency, and the damage caused directly or indirectly to their parents' generation, they are doing all they can to be flexible, diverse, and more loyal to themselves than to any company. The research says they place more value on material wealth than boomers, are more competitive, and work hard—as they are determined to take control of their future instead of leaving it in the hands of others. Xers are going to work in many jobs—staying as long as necessary in each to accumulate what they desire for a better life—their measure of success.

More advice is given on maintaining a good attitude and constantly remaining in touch with how you really feel about your work life from Carol Kleiman. It is all about being positive and "making lemonade out of lemons" when you are forced to accept a job in a new company—perhaps at a lower salary.

"It wasn't exactly what she wanted. It didn't pay as much as the one she had before. But she knew that just getting her foot in the door of the new company was all she needed. 'I'll prove my self so valuable,' she told me, 'that they'll want to keep me on and even pay me more.' It's up to you to put the squeeze on those lemons you were handed. And a good way to approach your present job is to be in touch with your own needs and hopes and dreams, if not on a daily, at least on a weekly, basis. Examining yourself about the health of your present job will help you diagnose how close your work 'temperature' is to 'normal.'

Questions to Ask Yourself
- What are the aspects of my job that appeal to me, that make me want to go to work each day?

- I like to feel I'm an important contributor. What do I accomplish each day that satisfies me?
- Now that I'm an insider, do I work for an ethical company, one I consider honorable?
- Am I being used to my fullest potential?
- While I know that salaries will be fairly low for the foreseeable future, can I live with—and on—what I'm making?
- If I do my present job well, will I be able to move ahead?
- Are my colleagues supportive? Do they include me in their conversations and get-togethers?
- Is this company open about its financial status? I don't want to get burned again.
- Is management aware I'm here? Do supervisors and executives go out of their way to say hello and make me feel welcome?
- Is my workload one I can handle?

If you answer yes to most of these questions, then your work 'temperature' is healthy, and you also have a head start on succeeding in your job and holding on to it. But at this point, precise affirmations and negative responses are only a daily guide, not a permanent record of your strengths and weaknesses as reflected in your present job. Instead, the questions are ones you have to keep asking yourself on a regular basis so you constantly are in touch with how you really feel about your work life.

They'll also clearly indicate to you how your employer feels about you."[21]

Another key to maintaining ongoing employment, or if you are just starting out in the business world trying to find your first job, is to be flexible. This means get a broad-based education and be willing to try almost anything as far as jobs or special projects are concerned. Look to temporary or part-time work to get a feel for a company or position. Don't get into a mind-set that there is only one job that's for you because (as was noted in Chapter One) while baby boomers work an average of 3-5 jobs in their careers, it is projected that Gen Xers will work in 10-15, and Gen Y's 25 or more. We are going to be in a lean economy (perhaps) for years, so the younger generations are going to have to be prepared at all times for their next gigs. I've read where as much as a third of new graduating classes will join the unemployed ranks in the next 10 years—not a pretty picture.

Each down business cycle in history is typically followed by a spurt of solid hiring growth. Companies have to build themselves back up in order to grow and satisfy demand after years of trimming back and releasing individuals, with skill sets that were perhaps too narrow. The upside is that they will be hiring a broad range of workers with more flexible skills. But as is occurring after the Great Recession, businesses remain cautious and will for quite some time. They will bring in a higher percentage of contingent workers—temps and consultants—in temp-to-perm positions. This is a growing trend, as companies want to evaluate workers in "trial periods" to determine they meet their needs without long-term commitments. It's not all bad for the employees—giving them a chance to get a feel for the company, its culture and management, and determine if the job is right for them.

What does the future hold for the nation's workers? Are the majority going to be temporary or contingent workers, without the security of full-time employment with benefits? There are many estimates about the temporary industry and the size of the temporary workforce. Regardless, the trend toward temp-to-perm is real, and the corporate continuous right-sizing phenomenon—which includes replacing full-time workers with contingent employees—is here to stay.

Charles Handy saw the future in his book *The Age of Unreason,* which was noted in the Chapter One, and was right on target.

His prediction that by 2000 half the working population would be making a living outside traditional organizations seemed crazy in the early 1980s.

Handy has provided some of the classic management ideas of the past decade, including the shamrock organization, the doughnut principle, and the portfolio career. The first gave companies a blueprint for identifying core activities and outsourcing everything else.

The second helped management and workers distinguish between the essential parts of a job or career -- by somewhat strange logic identified as the hole in the doughnut -- and the discretionary parts. The third encouraged workers not to think of their current jobs as a career but as just one part of a lifetime portfolio of wages, contract fees, charity work, and study.

To avoid the growing uneasiness inside and outside companies, Handy says, we must apply what he calls upside-down thinking, which he defines as an unconventional view of the future that stands everything we think we know on its head. When we were all employed, he says, we basically sold our time for money. So as long as we were doing what we wanted to do, the point of our lives was to get as much money for it as possible. Money was the measure of our success. In that world, education was primarily for a fixed time, and then it ended. The government provided certain benefits.

Upside-down thinking says that all these certainties will soon be dead. Governments are going broke and can't afford benefits. Education will have to become never-ending. Corporate taxes will go up if companies don't recognize their role in training and education. Because they can take nothing for granted -- including jobs -- workers will need to learn how to value time as well as money. If society is to absorb all this change without undue turmoil, nothing short of a revolution is needed in Western ways of capitalism, including in higher education, corporate law, and finance."[22]

One of the major changes in the workplace is the impact of technology and its rapid implementation. Computers, robotics, and other automated systems are going to be more and more depended upon to boost productivity in the future. (And the future is now.) Being proactive and keeping up-to-date on the latest programs, communication devices, and automation will make you more valuable to your employer.

Valerie Sokoloshy, a noted author and keynote speaker based in Dallas, offers a test to determine your aptitude on adding value to your job and company in "How To Be a Valued Employee." Even with downsizing and workplace revisions, this is an age of unprecedented possibilities. Take this quiz to see if you're ready to seize the opportunities change creates.

1. Continuing to do your work in the same way could result in:
   a. Burnout.
   b. A feeling of accomplishment.
   c. Getting left behind.

2. Setting business goals that are difficult to reach may cause:
    a. More impressive results.
    b. Frustration
    c. Guaranteed promotion.

3. Being a trustworthy team member helps the work group because:
    a. It creates more open and honest communication.
    b. It shows others your values.
    c. It shows your leadership skills.

4. When you are trying to solve a problem and are faced with constraints, you should:
    a. Ask more questions.
    b. Be more innovative.
    c. Take more time to gather data.

5. A "can-do" attitude helps you:
    a. Have strength to persevere when things get tough.
    b. Keep a smile on your face.
    c. Receive recognition as someone who can be trusted to get results.

6. With more work to do and fewer resources, attack your daily tasks by:
   a. Delegating your work.
   b. Doing only one thing at a time.
   c. Speeding up.

7. Without job security, you should focus your energy on your "employability," which means:
   a. Having skills to move to other departments.
   b. Your appeal to the job market.
   c. Your desire to do a good job.

8. If your work group needs to come up with breakthrough solutions, it should:
   a. Brainstorm with the boss.
   b. Search the Web for new ideas.
   c. Value different perspectives.

9. The "information age" requires different skills and behaviors, including:
   a. More technical expertise.
   b. Higher education with diverse degrees.
   c. People skills.

10. Whatever your career, what counts is your performance, which means:
    a. How long you have been in your job.
    b. What value you add to the organization.
    c. Your ability to perform in front of a group.

QUIZ ANSWERS (Each correct answer is worth ten points)

1. c. The world is changing so fast that doing the same things the same way is probably ineffective. Continually look for new ways that could bring different and better results.

2. a. When you set "stretch" goals, it can lead to greater gains and greater satisfaction. Don't allow yourself to settle for the norm. Push for going beyond the status quo.

3. a. When there is a climate of trust in the workplace, there is opportunity for a collaborative environment and mutual respect.

4. b. Being faced with limitations is more often the way it is. So, use limitations to apply creative, new, and better solutions rather than wasting energy worrying about conditions that will not change.

5. a. Enthusiasm provides energy to carry you forward and the emotional strength to take necessary risks.

6. c. The reality is that organizations are moving quickly to meet marketplace demands. You, too, must operate with a sense of urgency in everything you do. There is no time to wait for instructions or complain about the many roles you have. Instead, manage your daily activities by prioritizing them and then attacking them with gusto.

7. b. Employability means you are highly marketable with skills that can be transferred to a new work environment and are kept current.

8. c. Innovation can come from places other than your organization and from people different from you. Take time to learn how things are accomplished in other industries. Get input from a variety of sources. Be open to feedback from customer groups.

9. c. With the speed and complexity of changes in the workplace, the soft skills are more important. People do business with people they like and trust. People work more efficiently when there is collaboration. Relationships are built on people skills,

not technical skills.

10. b. What organizations pay for is the contribution and the performance that you bring to the workplace.

Quiz Scoring
Your score:

80-100: You clearly are one who anticipates the future and prepares for it with new skills and a positive outlook. You understand the need to learn continually and to lead by example whatever your level.

60-70: You must develop different ways of working and increase your employability by adding new skills.

Below 60: Take a clue. Don't be complacent and expect the organization to reward you for past performance or longevity in your job. Get committed to be the best you can be, which can be a motivator to your morale.[23]

When you're starting out in a company, keep in mind that the things you do are building your foundation in the organization and sending key messages to your coworkers, managers and customers. What is one of the most important steps you can take to "position" yourself in the company? To show that you take initiative, which is working outside the traditional role of your job. More and more you will see work that doesn't mesh neatly with someone's job description. This work will only get done when people muscle up to the bar and take on these new tasks, along with their existing workload. Those who step up to the challenge are the star performers. It's not enough to just take initiative and in doing things well – beyond your job description. It's also taking risks when necessary and seeing tasks through to completion. This will differentiate you from average performers.

In summary, you must be "change able" and grow intellectually to thrive and survive, because we have learned that we can no longer count on companies, the educational institutions, or government to take care of us. Corporations have recently been likened to dysfunctional families. You can pick up and leave headaches at one job only to run into similar problems at another. Do your due diligence on any potential employer. Check out their long-term stability and management team. Talk to former employees (find them through LinkedIn) because they will give unbiased insight you won't get from a recruiter selling you on the company. If you decide to make a change, you might try a smaller company. That is where the most opportunity lies today: Small businesses have been creating most of the new jobs for decades and, to note, women are starting two thirds of all new small businesses these days!

You have to be flexible, to do what is asked of you within moral and legal boundaries by employers. Be confident enough in yourself to accept a lateral move or a lesser title. Always jump at the opportunity for retraining programs. Be prepared to do contracted, project, or temporary work—that is what the future holds—so be equipped to represent yourself, your brand, as your company.

Create an environment where teamwork and harmony are encouraged and rewarded in your places of employment or contingent work. Learn to be forward thinking and recognize what's going on around you. Continually look for better, more efficient ways to perform work to add value to each process you are involved in. You should continue to educate and reeducate yourself and network with the people in your industry and community, who have the knowledge and the will to understand you and be your mentors. Embrace new workplace technologies. You should keep yourself physically fit so that you can handle whatever task or career change comes your way. Like it or not, a physically fit person is more likely to get hired over an unfit candidate—other things being equal. You should remain relatively debt free so that you can weather any change that you are forced to endure. If you do not evolve, you will always be at the mercy of our employers, government, or others, and this will impair your ability to take risks or make changes when you know they are necessary. You must act <u>now</u> to be prepared for the future—for your own preparedness is your only security going forward.

The following chapters are a series of articles written and published by the author for employment Web sites all related to the 5 Necessary Skills To Keep Your Career On Track.

CHAPTER 8

Where Will the New Jobs Come From?

The American economy has been gradually regaining strength since the Great Recession and, in due course, the sorely needed new jobs will follow. But what occupations will return the strongest, adding the greatest number of employees? Economists don't have the best news – forecasting jobs will follow in two broad categories of approximate equal proportions: professionals/specialized fields with bigger paychecks and lower-skill, lower paying jobs. The higher-end positions will be engineers, biomedical researchers, lawyers, network systems analysts, whereas the lower paying positions will be telemarketing representatives, sales clerks, home care providers, and similar. It appears that the forecast is lackluster for those in the middle—the office administrators, retail managers, and postal workers. When will any of these positions really "open up" in big numbers is the underlying question?

The Labor Department says nearly all of the new jobs will be in the service sector. The 78 million baby boomers will need more health care services, as they get older, is one example of sector growth. Other high technology jobs brought about by innovation—things we haven't even thought of yet—and alternative energy will likely add many higher paying jobs in more specialized fields.

The positions that disappeared such as construction workers, mortgage appraisers, loan officers, real estate agents, furniture makers, and manufacturing jobs may never come back in big numbers, especially the latter, with lower skilled manufacturing jobs heading off shore.

What retraining of workers will have to take place for these jobs and who will do the training? What additional course-work will be required to prepare those just entering the workforce? What regions of the country will emerge as the recipient of these jobs and what migration of workers will be required – so they are in the right place at the right time?

According to the Bureau of Labor Statistics (BLS), there are about 15 million people unemployed totaling just under ten-percent of the 154 million person labor force. It is important to note that this figure does not include the approximately 11 million people who have either expend-ed all unemployment benefits and/or have given up look-ing for jobs - many out of work for years. So the critical challenge will be to match up as many of these 26 million workers (in total) and the new entrants to the labor pool each year (which number about 1.5 million) to these jobs, in the locations where they will emerge.

The BLS projects the 2008-2018 Fastest-Growth Occupations:

	CHANGE EMPLOYMENT (000) 2008-2018			
	2008	2018	Number	Percent
Biomedical engineers	16.0	27.6	11.6	72.02
Network systems and data communications analysts	292.0	447.8	155.8	53.36
Home health aides	921.7	1382.6	460.9	50.01
Personal and home care aides	817.2	1,193.0	375.8	45.99
Financial examiners	27.0	38.1	11.1	41.16
Medical scientists, except epidemiologists	109.4	153.6	44.2	40.36
Physician assistants	74.8	103.9	29.2	38.99
Skin care specialists	38.8	53.5	14.7	37.86
Biochemists and biophysicists	23.2	31.9	8.7	37.42
Athletic trainers	16.3	22.4	6.0	36.95
Physical therapist aides	46.1	62.8	16.7	36.29
Dental hygienists	174.1	237.0	62.9	36.14
Veterinary technologists and technicians	79.6	108.1	28.5	35.77
Dental assistants	295.3	400.9	105.6	35.75
Computer software engineers, applications	514.8	689.9	175.1	34.01
Medical assistants	483.6	647.5	163.9	33.9
Physical therapist assistants	63.8	85.0	21.2	33.28
Veterinarians	59.7	79.4	19.7	32.95
Self-enrichment education teachers	253.6	334.9	81.3	32.05
Compliance officers, except agriculture, construction, health and safety, and transportation	260.2	341.0	80.8	31.05
Occupational therapist aides	7.8	10.2	2.4	30.74
Environmental engineers	54.3	70.9	16.6	30.62
Pharmacy technicians	326.3	426.0	99.8	30.57
Computer software engineers, systems software	394.8	515.0	120.2	30.44
Survey researchers	23.4	30.5	7.1	30.36
Physical therapists	185.5	241.7	56.2	30.27
Personal financial advisors	208.4	271.2	62.8	30.13
Environmental engineering technicians	21.2	27.5	6.4	30.1
Occupational therapist assistants	26.6	34.6	7.9	29.78
Fitness trainers and aerobics instructors	261.1	337.9	76.8	29.41

BLS projected 2008-2018 Largest Number of Jobs Added by Occupations:

	EMPLOYMENT (000)		CHANGE 2008-2018	
	2008	2018	Number	Percent
Registered nurses	2,618.7	3,200.2	581.5	22.20
Home health aides	921.7	1,382.6	460.9	50.01
Customer service representatives	2,252.4	2,651.9	399.5	17.74
Combined food preparation and serving workers, including fast food	2,701.7	3,096.0	394.3	14.59
Personal and home care aides	817.2	1,193.0	375.8	45.99
Retail salespersons	4,489.2	4,863.9	374.7	8.35
Office clerks, general	3,024.4	3,383.1	358.7	11.86
Accountants and auditors	1,290.6	1,570.0	279.4	21.65
Nursing aides, orderlies, and attendants	1,469.8	1,745.8	276.0	18.78
Postsecondary teachers	1,699.2	1,956.1	256.9	15.12
Construction laborers	1,248.7	1,504.6	255.9	20.49
Elementary school teachers, except special education	1,549.5	1,793.7	244.2	15.76
Truck drivers, heavy and tractor-trailer	1,798.4	2,031.3	232.9	12.95
Landscaping and groundskeeping workers	1,205.8	1,422.9	217.1	18.00
Bookkeeping, accounting, and auditing clerks	2,063.8	2,276.2	212.4	10.29
Executive secretaries and administrative assistants	1,594.4	1,798.8	204.4	12.82
Management analysts	746.9	925.2	178.3	23.87
Computer software engineers, applications	514.8	689.9	175.1	34.01
Receptionists and information clerks	1,139.2	1,312.1	172.9	15.18
Carpenters	1,284.9	1,450.3	165.4	12.87
Medical assistants	483.6	647.5	163.9	33.90
First-line supervisors/managers of office and administrative support workers	1,457.2	1,617.5	160.3	11.00

Network systems and data communications analysts	292.0	447.8	155.8	53.36
Licensed practical and licensed vocational nurses	753.6	909.2	155.6	20.65
Security guards	1,076.6	1,229.1	152.5	14.16
Waiters and waitresses	2,381.6	2,533.3	151.6	6.37
Maintenance and repair workers, general	1,361.3	1,509.2	147.9	10.86
Physicians and surgeons	661.4	805.5	144.1	21.79
Child care workers	1,301.9	1,443.9	142.1	10.91
Teacher assistants	1,312.7	1,447.6	134.9	10.28

Source: US Bureau of Labor Statistics 2011 http://www.bls.gov[24]

It is interesting to note that 10 out of the top 20 fastest-growth jobs are related to healthcare, again, most likely related to the aging of baby boomers.

There is some good news in that many of the occupations that will add the most new jobs are "people" related, e.g. healthcare, retail sales, customer service, office clerks, etc., which will be added in large, urban centers and will not necessitate the costly movement of people from across the country. The "specialty" professions may require a move, but moving costs are more likely to be reimbursed by the recruiting company. Twelve of the professions, with the highest growth rates, will require associate or higher degrees. So unemployed or underemployed workers may want to consider adding a degree or certification to their resume and set their sites on one of these fields of fast-growth fields that interest them. Although, this may be much easier said than done, as it's difficult to pay for more education when you are at the rock bottom of your earning potential working part-time or having gone through a stretch of unemployment. There may be some government grant money available for retraining under one of the current jobs stimulus programs.

All employees in the future are going to have to be more "proactive" than they have been previously. You will go nowhere slowly by just saying "it would be wonderful to be a Network Systems Analyst with all those new jobs being added," but then not to start any training for the position and hope you hear about a local position opening up. You must research an occupation first, for its' range of opportunities, and then set a goal to get the required education completed. You should also focus on a specific organization (or three or four) and perhaps get to know them (by taking a lesser or temporary position). This will give you much needed visibility with them as well.

The rule of all job searches today is to network with colleagues, former colleagues, classmates, trade association members, and civic organizations to learn of opportunities in field(s) of your interest and in the area you want to live. In the networks you develop, there is bound to be someone who knows an insider in a company you have targeted. Your resume can be presented to the recruiting department head and not just be placed in a (electronic) stack of the hundreds received.

There is an entrepreneur in many of us and many of the professions listed provide new opportunities for small companies or employment contracts. These include the fast growing occupations of computer consulting, network administration, home health aides, personal and home care aides, information technology, and others. The large company trend of outsourcing services gives you the opportunity to create a new business around one of these services, where you have expertise.

There are roughly 25 million businesses in the US. This breaks down to about 27,000 with over 500 employees - using the US Dept. of Labor's criteria combining large and medium-sized businesses. The remainder or roughly 24,975,000 are considered small businesses with less than 500 workers. The 27,000 large and medium sized businesses aren't creating new jobs and have not, in the aggregate, for the past couple of decades. In fact, layoffs are still occur, on and off, in these segments.

The "sweet spot" where jobs have been created and traditionally pulled us out of recessions is small business. Let's take a closer look at the small business segment breakdown. The majority of small businesses, or roughly 19 million, are sole proprietorships and self-employed individuals. This leaves roughly 6 million small businesses with multiple employees and is the segment we need to "turn on" to keep the economy moving in a positive mode.

During the Great Recession, small businesses did an unprecedented amount of belt-tightening just to keep their doors open. This worked. Productivity increased a phenomenal 6 percent as we emerged from the doldrums.

Companies big and small learned to do more with less. But before hiring really kicks into high gear, there has to be confidence in the sustained growth of the economy. Understandably these companies don't want to overextend the liabilities side of their balance sheets by adding workers prematurely.

Our government needs to come to the realization of this "sweet spot" of jobs creation and carve out tax increase legislation for these small business owners, who are not the rich "fat cats" tax laws seem to suggest. It will only continue to exacerbate the new jobs creation quandary if we cannot treat a small business owner differently than the true rich crowd. An extra $500,000 in the hands of a small business entrepreneur is likely to increase his or her workforce. When a small business owner starts to feel comfortable with their business and earnings, and sees the opportunity expansion will bring, they hire new employees.

You have to take charge of your own career. As Jack Welch, former Chairman and CEO of GE stated, "Take charge of your career or someone else will." Many experts have predicted that we may not see 5% unemployment for several years – perhaps not even until the end of the decade. So competition will be fierce for jobs. It is more important than ever to be proactive in planning, networking, and getting the best educational experience you can - for securing your next gig. Workers in the future are going to have many jobs and need to understand they are going to always have to be contemplating "the next" opportunity.

CHAPTER 9

How To Speed The New Job Process Along: A 90 Plan

While there is no silver-bullet available to get you back into the full-time workforce, there are proven methods that will expedite the process. The rule of thumb for the time to find a job (and it has held true during most of the last decade) is one month for each $10,000 of annual income you have earned. For example, if you made $90,000 in your last job it will take you roughly nine months to find comparable employment, a year if you made $120,000, etc. But things are different as we're moving forward in the '10's decade. While we are in a recovery, don't expect the job market to return to the way it was a few years back.

We now realize how fragile our national economy is; how closely tied we are to the world's economy; and that our government cannot jump in and "save the day," as we have witnessed its inability to create jobs other than government jobs. And on this last point, that is exactly what we do not need - a bigger, bloated government, which created a national debt greater than the combined debt of all the other countries of the world - sapping available funds from the credit markets that are sorely needed for private enterprises to grow and add jobs.

The jobs growth engine of our economy for the past two decades has been small business, which (depending on the source you follow) has created between 70 and 80 percent of all new jobs. It can be argued that this growth came as large corporations downsized and outsourced more and more of their functions. Regardless, this trend will continue as these corporations become even more risk adverse.

The first thing needed to fast track your job search is to re-tool your resume. Keep in mind it's not about you - but about the skills required by a potential employer, with your skill set overlaid to determine the most qualified candidate. You will want to tweak your resume to mesh with the unique job requirements of each position you are interested in. You've heard it before but it's worth repeating - always maintain an up-to-date resume. The last thing you want is for a friend or colleague to "open a door" for you and ask for your resume, then not receive it for a week or two. It needs to be in their hands while you are in top-of-mind awareness.

I will bet that just about everyone reading this article can find a volunteer position directly or indirectly related to their past employment, within one week. If you have financial services experience, volunteer with a community agency to help people repair their credit scores, as an example. With a human resources background you could assist in a job services center helping workers get back into the labor force. Construction workers would be welcome at Habitat for Humanity. Who knows, you might end up pounding nails with a CEO or city councilmen - not bad connections to do some networking. There are three primary reasons to volunteer: It gives you a "story" to tell a potential employer about what you've been doing; it may provide the opportunity to network and find a new job; and it will build up your self-esteem - utilizing your skills and doing what you do best - giving you the confidence you need to project, as you land interviews.

Networking is where you will find your next job. I do not mean to rush out and join Twitter and see how many followers you can get in 60 days, or friends and family on MySpace or Facebook. That is not sophisticated networking - just because someone's name showed up. But do join LinkedIn, the most professional social networking site, if you have not already done so. Use your newly crafted resume to fill out your profile and search for friends, classmates, and former colleagues to re-connect with. You do not want to appear desperate. Don't ask for a job. Ask about what they are doing. Offer any help you can in getting them connected to others for their own careers or for a work project. Tell them about your volunteer work while you are looking for a new career position. Let them offer to assist you. This is effective networking.

Don't waste a great deal of time on job search sites, which are more or less the "help wanted ads" of the digital age. You can find sites that will let you drill down for a particular field and by city and region, but you will be competing with hundreds or even thousands of others for these positions. Do research on the companies which employ people with your skills - by reading annual reports, searching their web sites, trade associations, press releases, etc. Then use LinkedIn or similar professional sites to find out which ones are hiring; current and former employees you or one of your connections might know; and who can make an introduction for you to get directly to the hiring manager. This is the best way to ensure you will be brought in for an interview.

With small businesses adding three-quarters of all new jobs, focus your efforts on those which may have been the recipient of outsourced business in your field or a closely related one. You may very well find that one of the large corporations you contact now outsources what your specialty is. Ask whom they outsource it to - perhaps get them to forward your resume to them (a great way to open the door). When connecting with a small business use your large corporate experience to your advantage by suggesting how you can get more companies to outsource to them.

It can be argued that one-half of all jobs are now filled with contingent workers - consultants, contract, or temporary employees. Find a staffing company or two, specializing in your field, and let them go to work and find you an interim position either in your field or closely related. Over a third of these jobs become full-time employee positions -- and you get the opportunity to experience the company's culture firsthand and they see how you blend in with their existing workforce.

While there are no guarantees in life, following these steps can stack the deck in your favor to land a new job in the shortest time possible. Good luck!

CHAPTER 10

Women Overtake Men As The Dominant Gender Of The Workforce

Guess what gents? Your favored status in the business world recently came to a screeching halt. Look around you - on business flights, in executive meetings, on project teams and you see as many women as men. That's right, no more majority rule.

The US Labor Department has predicted that men will be surpassed by women as the majority of the US workforce this Fall - no one knows the day or the hour (and it's only as accurate as their statistical sampling) but may be happening as you read this article. Women held 49.83% of jobs in June and have continued to gain on men. Of the 7.2 million jobs lost since the beginning of the last recession, about three quarters were men cut from traditional male dominated industries. Whereas women have experienced job increases in education, local government, and healthcare where they have been in the plurality. In Canada, women solidly hold the majority of jobs with 50.6%. US women also hold over 250,000 more second jobs than men and 6 million more part-time jobs (which should have already pushed them over the one-half mark).

The days of the senior (male) executive taking the rising young (male) star under his wing in the classic mentoring scenario are rapidly disappearing. With women catching the workplace by storm, companies have begun to realize women are going to occupy more of their corner offices in the very near future. Many have wised up and formed company wide mentoring programs to give equal attention to women and minorities - and their executives have been told to get out of their comfort zones to bring the next generation of leaders into the fold.

Sure the good old boy network still controls the top posts, but not for long. According to the National Center for Education Statistics bachelor degrees are now earned by a ratio of 4-to-3 in favor of women and they predict that will increase to 3 women for every 2 men by 2017. And women are now receiving more advanced degrees than men. The boys club still skews the salary scale. Women who worked full time earned only 80 percent of what their male counterparts earned, and 77 percent when part-time positions are also factored in. Part of this disparity is because men still control the ranks and higher pay of executive level positions. But nonetheless, there still exists a disturbing gender pay disparity and experts believe it still may be decades before gender equality in pay is finally achieved.

As women grab the reins of senior management, they must learn strong communication skills and develop more opportunities to gain the cooperation of other executives - since they are, relatively speaking, outsiders crashing through the glass ceilings. They have not been led down the path like many of their male counterparts. The latter helped along by senior executives to establish credibility and trust with other key influencers in the company. Women have been largely on their own to create alliances, develop rapport, and a positive perception by others.

It's a new world out there - expedited along out of the throws of the deepest recession most of us have known - embrace it with open arms.

CHAPTER 11

Keeping The Job You Have – Much Easier Than Finding A New One

Whether you've unemployed, underemployed, long-term in a position, or looking for a career change you will need to master some business and life skills to progress in your career.

The philosopher and poet, Dante writes in the 12th Century: The secret of getting things done is to act! This is the same lesson carried forward by Stephen R. Covey in many of his books - what he coins as proactivity. You, and only you, are ultimately responsible for your career. To leave something this important in the control of a manager, with many other interests and employees, a company, a union, school or to only react to circumstances that befall you can be a mistake of a life time. The best advice in the world won't do you any good unless you take the information and proactively do something with it.

In my book, I outlined the critical skills to survive and to get ahead in the toughest of employment markets. You must develop the ability to be cognizant of your surround-ings - of your co-workers next door and your boss in the corner office - but also your company, industry, products, competitors, and the health of the local and national economy. This will make you a more knowledgeable and useful employee and give you the insight to better position yourself and company in the marketplace. If you are looking for a job or wanting to make a career change, you need to research what occupations are growing and what companies are positioned to prosper. No use becoming a deckhand on a sinking ship or venturing into a shrinking, dead-end industry.

Being proactive will assist in all of your business and career endeavors; whether its getting that report out on time, contemplating your customers' needs, or implementing a beneficial, new procedure before your boss mandates it. It's recognizing changes in your industry or organization that aren't positive for you personally or your company - and to start the process to make a change, on your timetable and terms. It is to be continually educated and re-educated in your chosen profession and the economic outlook in general. If you are not gaining knowledge on new and changing processes, you are actually slipping backward and losing your competitive edge to contemporaries.

Learning to deal with many management styles and degrees of professionalism (or lack thereof) will give you an edge over your co-workers. You need to develop honest and straightforward dialog with bosses, so you know their expectations for you. Getting along with other employees in your workplace is going to be a challenge at times. Recognizing cultural differences and unique work styles and keeping communications open and positive will only help. Complex jobs, especially in the era of downsizing where new tasks have been handed to the survivors, have made it critical to work well with others to get projects completed. If a boss becomes unbearable to deal with, only you will know when its time to move on to another company. But if you are still gaining valuable knowledge and progressing in the company, you might want to hold on a little longer until timing is right for a change - when you have another position lined up.

A mentor can be very beneficial in advancing your career. Mentors aren't just people in more senior levels within your company, but can be life coaches, ministers, family friends, or colleagues from a professional association. They may be able to assist you to navigate the corporate "landmines" and position you to move ahead in your organization or help in a quest for a new job. The more information you have at your disposal, and the ability to bounce things off another and get a second opinion, the better equipped you are to handle challenges that arise. Many companies now have formal mentoring programs, but even without one more tenured employees are likely willing to take you under their wings if asked sincerely.

Networking with industry colleagues, old college

friends, professional associations, church groups, or any potential employers will increase your knowledge of the job market and improve your marketability. Social networks are mediums to connect with others but still must be used effectively to develop into good networking relationships. LindedIn is, in my opinion, the best professional site. But remember the cardinal rule of networking - you have to give before you receive. You are taking care of yourself, your career, and building your self-esteem all at the same time by maintaining contact with friends and colleagues. Networking is the most efficient way of finding a new job or to get promoted in your existing company.

Many people are only reactive, and sit back expecting someone else to look after their interests, when a monkey wrench gets tossed into their career. Often the damage is done and it's too late to repair the situation. The people who have the best careers are the ones who are proactive and stay ahead of the game - the go-to people in their organizations - who know how to get projects completed 100% of the time. The key is to acquire all of the knowledge you can about an organization, its management, and its products/services then act on the information. If you are currently working for that organization and prospects don't look good long-term start making a plan to move on. Conversely, only apply for positions in companies that are well-managed and in growth industries. Do your homework - then act on it!

CHAPTER 12

I Hate My Job (But Doing Nothing About It) – Only You Can Take Charge Of Your Career

How many times have you heard a friend, colleague, or relative say "I hate my job?" It seems to be a reoccurring topic with many people - one that can be very tiresome. "I only have ten years to retirement and I can't wait to get out of this place." "I despise my boss - I know she is out to get me." "This job totally stresses me out, it's ruining my life." There are many variations but it's the same old theme. You can't help but recognize the tone of helplessness in their voices. Is it a societal issue that we are not responsible for what happens to us, somebody else always has to bear the blame?

Too often we cruise on autopilot and accept what a company or job gives us. Especially in today's tough job market, you will hear "jobs are scarce and I can't afford to risk making a change." But these are usually the same people who complain a lot, and shoulder stress, without taking action even in prosperous times. Stephen R. Covey states, "Many people wait for something to happen or someone to take care of them. But the people who end up with the good jobs are the proactive ones who are solutions to problems, not problems themselves, who seize the initiative to do whatever is necessary, consistent with correct principles, to get the job done."

Sarah Burgard, a sociologist at the University of Michigan, in an article published by LiveScience says "In fact, chronic job insecurity was a stronger predictor of poor health than either smoking or hypertension in one of the groups we studied." She goes on to say that "Based on how participants rated their own physical and mental health, we found that people who were persistently concerned about losing their jobs reported significantly worse overall health in both studies and were more depressed in one of the studies than those who had actually lost and regained their jobs recently."[25]

How can this be? When you think about it, the stress of the insecurity about the next paycheck, medical benefits, retirement plans - all tied to our jobs - has to take a toll. Almost everyone has a family member, friend, and or colleague either out of work or in fear of a forced career change and it's the major focus in much of the media we see. If you get laid off or otherwise terminated from your employment, at least you know where you stand and you can channel your anxiety into action to network and search for another job. Not that this is without its' own stressfulness but at least the uncertainty and helplessness of waiting for the ax to fall is relieved.

Does anyone really believe that they are going to get a tweet on Twitter, a FaceBook message, an email, or knock on the door stating, "we've been on an extensive search looking for someone just like you." The fact is you are responsible for your career choices. As Eleanor Roosevelt once said, "No one can hurt you without your consent." Only you have the power to be proactive and take the initiative to make a change, if change is needed. If you have a horrible boss or work environment, you have to take responsibility to either work with team members to improve the situation or start making plans to move on.

The key is to make a plan. This doesn't necessarily involve quitting your job. It may very well be setting your sights on a different position within your company and proactively going after that job. Don't do anything rash - half the battle is recognizing there is a problem - then developing a conscious plan to do something about it. This should be a written plan and shared with a trusted mentor or respected friend to get another viewpoint. You need to look within and determine what you really want to be doing. Because you can't have a real plan, until you establish the goal. What can you become totally immersed in and enjoy going to work to do? This is usually easier said than done. It must be practical and reasonably attainable, but nonetheless what you really have a vision of doing. We can't all venture off to Africa with the Peace Corp on a humanitarian mission, as we have other life commitments. It may require several intermediary steps, like going back to school for an advanced degree, getting a shorter term well-paying job to save money to start your own business, or getting an entry level job in the field of your dreams to allow you to work toward the position you desire.

Take control of your career (and life) by not accepting the status quo until it's too late. Life is too short!

CHAPTER 13

Writing an Effective Resume

There are hundreds of books and Internet sites with excellent information about resume writing, so I'm not going to reinvent the wheel here—and the resume has evolved quite dramatically in the digital information age both in content and delivery methods. But there is consensus about the concise, factual, clear character of the most impactful resumes.

When you have the experience of dealing with top corporate executives, or recruiters for key positions, you quickly learn that the quantity of letters, emails, and information (in general) reaching the people in these "focal point" positions is enormous. You learn that to be brief and concise will better the chances of your cover letter, memorandum, conversation, e-mail, or letter being read and/or acted upon. It's all about the executive summary. It is just what the name implies: a succinct synopsis of a report, plan, or activity that gives the key points or findings in the fewest words possible. It contains selective information the author deems important. A key executive's time is extremely valuable, and he or she will appreciate those who get their point across in as abbreviated a manner as possible. (Not Twitter brief though – get your complete point across.)

Time constraints also apply to busy human resources managers, recruiters, directors, and general managers when they go through a file of resumes. They don't want a lot of fluff – just the facts.

I recall going through a stack of 250 resumes for an open sales manager position and spending five to ten seconds on each cover letter and the same for resumes, unless something really caught my eye. My colleagues and professional recruiters tell me this is the norm and precisely the reason many companies use keyword scanning software today, since you can't possibly pay all resumes the attention they require. You thoroughly read them if you notice a particular company, job, skill, or perhaps school—but it has got to jump off the page. Cover letters, which have the specific aim of catching the reader's attention, are positioned to get your resume read – so always include one when sending out a resume.

The whole intent of a resume (and cover letter) is to get you in front of the person doing the hiring, for an interview. It must show how you are a qualified, suitable candidate based on the <u>exact</u> job description. You can expound on an objective, accomplishment, skill, or position once you get the interview.

As mentioned, many companies use keyword scanning software, which are the words used describing your work experience, education, and skills mastered. With the digital mega job boards, such as Monster, attracting thousands of resumes from all over the country (or world for that matter), many companies use keyword scanning software to narrow their searches for "exact fit" candidates for their available positions. It is important even if a company doesn't use keyword scanning, to mirror the position's keywords as closely as possible. Make certain (the job description) keywords are used throughout your resume especially in the opening section.

There are two schools of thought about a dedicated keyword section on your resume. For a human read only resume it certainly isn't necessary and if you have truly woven in the position's keywords throughout your resume many don't believe it is necessary – even for a scan version. It is important that the language of the resume is proper and flows correctly. If your resume passes the scan, a recruiter, hiring manager and others, will then read it. I have seen where candidates have tried to squeeze in every known keyword and it turns the language into nonsense—which isn't going to impress anyone. So craft it carefully.

Write your own resume because you know the "facts" better than anyone else, but have it tweaked by a professional who knows the ins and outs of keyword searches, so yours will survive the gauntlet to a real human review.

Writing your own resume draft will assist in self-awareness and give you more confidence to sell yourself—since you will have to explain each word and phrase in interviews—so it's wise to be well versed on exactly what is written. Also to note, you only have to go back 10 years for employment experience on your resume (the generally accepted rule). During an interview, they will want to know about your experience before that time, but the close-in relevant skills acquired and employment experience are the important pieces to get you in front of the interviewer.

Some people will argue that three or four pages are fine for a resume, but I go back to the example of the executive summary. Present only the pertinent information on two pages, if at all possible. Unless it's the greatest story ever told, it won't be read!

Your resume should be in a neat, block format, with headings highlighted for ease of reading. Even though most of your distribution will be via Internet, you will want a quality printed version for in-person interviews and for mailings. You can use bullets, bold type, and box in details to focus attention on key points. But on a resume to be sent over the Internet, since some programs don't translate these formats, verify what program to use. (Many organizations will specify this for their keyword scanning software to work.)

Most importantly, your resume must be customized for the unique job requirements of each job you are applying for by emphasizing your skills that are directly applicable.

I have received resumes with photographs at times – some with complete portfolios. There is even the trend to send a YouTube introduction of yourself, especially if applying for a position in another part of the country where an in-person interview wouldn't be possible right away. This may not be appropriate for most business situations unless you are applying for a position on camera, in modeling, or acting so save that for later in the interview process. If the prospective employer wants to see what you look like, he or she can schedule an interview and (be certain) they will check out your Facebook page.

Carol Kleiman, in *Winning the Job Game*, offers advice about resumes:

> Employers just want the facts. You can show your personality and even embellish your achievements in the job interview (and cover letter): A listing of where you worked and when, in chronological order starting with your most recent job must follow the opening, the skills you have acquired, as supporting evidence. This is then followed by your educational credentials and is the Number One resume format for today's market. But the preferred resume doesn't work for everyone, especially people who have been out of the job market for long periods of time and those who have changed jobs frequently.

> For the latter, a possible alternative is the functional

resume. It prominently lists your skills, pertinent experience, and names of employers but omits the dates you worked for them. There is nothing devious about this form of resume, even if it isn't the most popular one. It gets the job done. And you can give more detailed information in the job interview, which you probably would not get if you sent in a chronological resume.

Tell the truth. While it's a sin to tell a lie under any circumstances, lying on your resume is the worst thing you can do. Not only is it wrong, but also you'll be found out. Smart employers – and you don't want to work for any other kind – carefully check out all job applicants they're interested in. They don't want to hire anyone with questionable characteristics, and they'll look into everything you say – remember, they're in no hurry to hire in uncertain economic times. They want to learn about your credit rating and police record and whether you pay your taxes. They may also find out that you do not have a master's degree in esoteric foreign languages as you claimed you do on your resume.[26]

Most knowledgeable employment professionals now state that the traditional chronological resume of latest skills mastered, jobs held, and education completed is outdated. Relevant professional skills acquired say more about a person's qualification for any given job. But I agree with Carol Kleiman in the fact that companies still want to see the your tenure (in jobs) and want all time accounted for in your career to date. For this reason, first note professional skills that apply <u>exactly</u> to the position you are seeking. Then list employment and educational experience from most recent to previous, supported by dates. Not to list previous jobs in this manner, as some resume writers suggest, will cause most readers to think you are hiding (or lacking) something.

I agree with the professionals that "titles" do not carry the weight they once did – employers want to see what you have accomplished, and the skills mastered, more than what your title was. Also, employers are much more accepting of movement from one company to another. A recruiter I spoke to recently describes her view of candidates' resumes and how she reads between the lines. First, she said she has gotten over the angst that job-hopping is so prevalent these days in the resumes she reads. If a candidate has reached an age (not legal to ask—but most recruiters can back into the number) and should be at a more stable time of his or her career, then she may question the moves more closely. More importantly, the positives of the candidate must outshine any negatives.

But don't be misled. Frequent job changes will be scrutinized. You still must prove you had accomplishments and achieved objectives in each position. Less than two years in a job is still a real question. You will be asked about why you changed jobs and if you left on good terms. As mentioned, you must account for all of your time on a resume. If you held a job for less than two or three months, you may want to leave it off—unless there is a really good reason for the short tenure. When interviewing, be up front and tell the truth. An example might be: a job better suited to my skills, which I had previous applied for, finally came through after I had accepted the other position.

A "combination type" of resume is probably the best to use in today's business climate: listing skills acquired, significant accomplishments, and chronological employment and educational experience. Education isn't just an "oh by the way" add on. Make sure you not only list your college degree(s) but other relevant courses, seminars, etc., to assure recruiters you are keeping up-to-date in your chosen field.

Tom Peters, one of the top authors and management gurus of our time, strongly believes we have to differentiate ourselves from the crowd to get noticed and be given opportunities in a new organization—or even your existing company. His belief is that each time you sit down with your boss for a performance review you need to detail your accomplishments (resume form) for the past year— showing a logical progression and increase in knowledge of your company, marketplace, and position.

Most important: Let me repeat—your strengths must align with the requirements of the position you are applying for. Ask for a detailed job description, to make no mistake. Experience suggests that if you avoid wordiness, keyword optimize, and follow an easy-to-read, visually appealing format, your resume will be read. There is one catch. You must pique the reader's interest with a striking cover letter—first.

CHAPTER 14

Cover Letters With Impact

The importance of cover letters cannot be overstated to grab the attention of a prospective employer and get your resume read:

Creating a succinct cover letter is a must. It's the bridge between what you have to offer and what the company wants. Its purpose is to make the hiring officer continue on and read your resume with interest. And the next step after that is your goal: being called in for a job interview. For years, I've asked employers which is more important to them, the resume or the cover letter. Most waffle on an answer and say both matter.

But when I question them further it becomes obvious that the cover letter is what makes them decide whether or not to read the resume itself. In a crowded field of applicants, the cover letter can make or break you: It's the first thing they see. And if it doesn't make you stand out from hundreds of other applicants, isn't impressive, or doesn't have any important facts in it, your resume probably will be deep-sixed.[27]

Just as an "executive summary" is very important to top executives, the cover letter is critical to busy managers, directors, or recruiters reviewing stacks of responses to employment advertisements or posts. Unless your letter grabs their attention, it isn't going to be read in detail. Do all possible to find out the name and title of the person doing the hiring and address it to him or her. Your letter will get much more attention than if it is labeled "To Whom It May Concern" or "Dear HR Director."

Your resume contains the *facts* about your experience. You can highlight accomplishments that apply to a particular job, but you must give factual information, in condensed form. Conversely, your cover letter, while it still should exhibit succinctness, gives you the opportunity to write exactly why *you* are the perfect person for the position. Avoid embellishment or flowery words. Use action verbs like: *created* company's social media strategy, *sold* services to twelve Fortune 100 companies, or *directed* integrated circuit design group.

Some employment specialists say your first sentence must refer to the job title and the site where you saw the job post. I disagree. That is a waste of the single most important position of the letter. You have got to hook the reader with the first line to get them to read further.

I completed a writing course many years ago that improved my writing skills dramatically. The instructor discussed the power of a captivating opening sentence and clean, concise language. He could read almost any letter and eliminate words while maintaining (even clarifying) the meaning. He had a rule, which I follow today, to begin each sentence by saying, "I want to tell you that"—then write your sentence. Example: I want to tell you that...

Cost-cutting strategies reduced expenses by 35% in the first year as general manager of my company's production group, with subsequent savings each year thereafter.

Then address the job posted and give a positive statement about your capability to handle it.

Complete the letter by noting other key points about how your unique skills and accomplishments can meet the needs of the employer. This is where you detail projects completed. Employment experts tell us that "projects" are as important today as jobs held used to be. Being part of a design team, for example, and completing a year-and-a-half project shows you can work with others and can finish what you start.

Another one of the lessons learned was to eliminate hackneyed phrases completely. Phrases like "enclosed herein," "regarding our conversation," "pursuant to your phone call," "at our meeting on March 15, 2011," or "attached please find" are overused, and slow down the flow of a letter or report. If something is attached or enclosed note "attachment" or "enclosure" at the bottom of the page. It is obvious that something is in the envelope with your letter. "According to our phone conversation" and "at the meeting dated..." are not necessary. If you just had a phone conversation or an earlier meeting with a person, she will remember it. Simply jump in and discuss what's on your mind about the previous exchange.

Close with a call to action: "I will call you at the beginning of next week to discuss this opportunity." It is better to leave the action in your court than with the other party. If you write, "Call me after you have reviewed this," then wait for weeks and receive no phone call, it goes against what you said in your letter if you now call. It can be annoying to someone reviewing hundreds of resumes and put them on the defensive. A typical response might be "I haven't had a chance to get back to you, because I've been in meetings; I'll do so when I have reviewed all of the candidates' resumes." (Don't bug me is the message!) Whereas, if you said you would follow up and call, then you can say, "I mentioned in my letter that I would follow up with you this week." This shows you are a person of your word and followed up as promised. You still may get the same response that "I haven't reviewed all of the candidates yet," but you are not forcing the reader to make an excuse for not doing something. Believe me, the tone of the conversation will be different, and the chances of a callback will be greater.

You might find the use of fax machines (old technology) to your advantage, because few others do so. Faxing a resume and cover letter may get your qualifications reviewed before the masses of e-mailed resumes (and more attention). If you fax a follow-up request, befriend an administrative assistant and tell him or her that you haven't been able to connect with (name) and you don't want to bother them by leaving phone messages, as you know they must be busy. Ask politely to have your fax picked up and carried to the person you are trying to reach. Make your fax short and sweet. Write that you know they must be very busy reviewing applicants, or the assistant said they had been in meetings, and emphasize that you are well-qualified for the position and would appreciate talking to them when they have a minute or two to spare. (This, of course, does not work if the company has specified only apply online.) But a follow up note can still be faxed. Even if your cover letter and resume had been passed over, it may cause them to reconsider.

The key is to get in the door so that you can expound on your professional skills and let your personality shine. That is the primary purpose of the cover letter and it must have your "fit" for the position jump off the page to the recruiter.

CHAPTER 15

Choose Your Career Advisor Wisely: Some "So-Called" Experts Just In It For The Money – No Real-World Experience

Career advice experts are popping up all over social and traditional media with varying claims of expertise. Many lack "real" experience in career counseling or employer/employee relations and are merely opportunistic. I do not believe there is ill intent with most, but I find bad advice or incomplete advice to be worse than no advice at all. I also have a real problem with those out to exploit unemployed people - many desperate - who are down to the last of their savings or unemployment benefits.

The only thing recession-proof in today's job market recovery is the career advice field, with seminars, publishers churning out career books, and personal coaching businesses springing up in every nook and cranny of the Internet. A story in a large metropolitan newspaper on one of these self-proclaimed experts goes something like this: Susan Smith (name changed) was a free-lance writer in the entertainment industry when her career hit the skids. She needed a career makeover and decided she was a career expert and used her writing skills to get a career advice book published and launched her own blog. Poof! Now she's a full blown career coach. And many of these self-proclaimed experts are commanding fees of $500 to $1500 a month per client - not bad for a brand new profession!

An example of an ill-conceived, half-baked article recently appeared on a top Internet jobs site. It goes through eight steps to "gift yourself employment." What a powerful concept - I wish I had thought of just gifting new jobs - it would save a great deal of effort.

Her first point, finding a job takes time and available space to conduct the search - she even suggests a local restaurant. The latter proposition is horrible advice. Restaurants are noisy, by definition you're not going to be organized well, and the restaurant and other patrons will love having you there (not). Set up a home office or a private room of a library where you can use the phone, without background noise. And finding a job will take time - a simply brilliant observation - but gives no clue about average times to find a job! Which, by the way, is roughly one month for each $10,000 of annual income you have earned e.g. eight months to replace an $80,000 job.

Second, you're going to face competition in today's tough job market - another stroke of genius. But she does offer some good advice about the possible use of your background skills and talent in a different field - thinking outside the box.

Third, put updating your resume on the "to do" list. Terrible advice. Until you update your resume and figure out your complete set of skills you can't even contemplate her advice of finding a related out of the box field to conduct your search. You can't post your resume (since it's outdated), send it to anyone, nor interview with it. This is job search 101 and the very first thing you must do. Get your resume up-to-date focusing on your skills and accomplishments and always keep it updated.

Fourth, "use social networks to, well, network." Social networking sites are strictly mediums to find names of other people, hopefully in related fields or who can connect you to potential new jobs. She says nothing about how to effectively network, which is building relationships with the people you meet online, offering to give them assistance, discovering similar interests, and common friends. This is networking. Just because you found someone's name online does not mean you can ask him or her for a job or to recommend you to someone else. This would be like meeting someone on the street and asking them for a job. A new online contact would be extremely foolish to recommend you to anyone until they know and trust you.

Fifth, post your resume. Not bad advice, but your resume should always be customized to highlight your skills (and key words) to the particular job you are going after. Posting your resume on job search sites is the electronic equivalent of sending your resume to help wanted newspaper ads of yesteryear - with thousands of competitors. Yes, creating your own Web site will help you to stand out - some good advice - but where you will most likely find a job is through effective networking not a job site. I have read where up to 90% of senior manager and higher jobs are not even posted outside the company and most likely involve a recruiter. This is where networking comes in to connect with someone inside a company who knows of a particular job, which is a good fit for your qualifications. Perhaps even getting your resume on a hiring manager's desk before anyone from the outside hears about it - eliminating competition.

Sixth, join career or job clubs. The camaraderie is good for moral support but they won't find you a job.

Seventh, hit the streets. This is some of her worst advice unless you are applying at Joe's Plumbing Supply. Professional businesses do not want you "dropping by" to hand deliver your resume, nor calling, and they state this in their HR Web sites.

Her eighth point, and last one, is probably her best - Consider something temporary. As she suggests, find a temporary employment firm that specializes in your field of work. Many times contingent work leads to full-time employment, but more importantly it gives you a story to tell potential employers about what you've been doing.

It shows them you are industrious, and willing to think outside the box.

My advice is to check out the backgrounds of career counselors before you buy their products or services. Find people with real-world experience and study their material first to see if what they espouse makes common sense. I've reviewed thousands of resumes and personally recruited and hired hundreds of people, and have a couple of decades of experience with large corporations and start-ups. My experience and what I believe I can do to help countless floundering people in this tough job market is the reason I wrote a book on careers - not I'll write a book and then become a career expert.

CHAPTER 16

Stressed Out Workers In Stagnant Careers – Cause or Effect?

Manpower, the job-placement firm, just released a survey which found that 84 percent of currently working adults plan to look for a new job in 2011 – this us up from 60 percent a year earlier – reports CNN. This is not surprising since research released early last year revealed that over one-half of the US workforce felt their careers had stagnated. This state of employment restlessness, with continuing high unemployment numbers and general economic uncertainty, is causing stress, anxiety, and even depression in many workers.

I talked to a couple a short time ago who described the stress and turmoil in their lives, from a round of layoffs occurring recently at his job, and now talk of a second round. He has worked for one of the largest defense contractors for eight years during an era of growth - but now uncertainty reigns under a new Congress and reductions in defense spending. The couple both echoes what's causing the almost debilitating stress - the fear of the unknown. "It's a good job and I don't want to walk away from it. Besides, in this job market, what else is out there?" says the stressed out husband. "Not knowing is almost worse than losing your job, at least then you know where you sit." When I asked what (they) were doing about it, I got the response "worrying a lot."

There isn't a "silver-bullet" to maintaining employment in any job market. But one thing is for certain: doing nothing isn't going to help. Frequently we are in a status quo mindset and accept most anything an organization puts forward. But just waiting for the ax to fall is one of the dumbest things you can do!

What happens to your job performance if you are at unhealthy stress levels? Your work suffers. You are not upbeat and lack motivation for your subordinates, teammates, and even customers. You probably have more sick days. This decline of positive contribution can even be your downfall - setting yourself up for a target in the next round of cutbacks and can be a self-fulfilling prophecy. Yes, the insecurity you feel in your job can cause you to lose it.

What can workers do to remove themselves from this vicious cycle? What can be done to mitigate the employment uncertainties to take some stress and anxiety out of your life? Are you (personally) staying up with the latest technology and keeping up-to-date from an educational standpoint, to be more proficient than your co-workers?

Are you a go-to person creating value for your company each and every day? You need to answer these questions and build a solid network both internally (within your company) and externally with peers in your industry and former colleagues. Help create a healthy work environment in your company where teamwork is encouraged and satisfaction is achieved. You should add value to each task you undertake. Always seize the opportunity to continuously re-educate yourself, and use your network of peers for their knowledge and guidance. You will gather valuable information about other departments or divisions in your company, where your experience would be a good fit, and where there is a position perhaps more stable than your present one. You will want to know about opportunities outside your company—should you have to make a change—and networking will give you insight into the broader marketplace. And always, always have an updated resume – highlighting your unique skills – ready for opportunities when presented.

Religiously build your savings account for a potential rainy day; this will add a great deal to your security and reduce anxiety. Being overly dependent on a company can destroy your ability to take risks or make changes even when you know they are necessary.

You can best prepare for the future by putting these practices in place. Taking charge of your own career will create your security going forward and help mitigate much of your angst and stress.

CHAPTER 17

Interviewing From a Position of Strength

We have all heard of the importance of first impressions. Many recruiters and executives I know tell me they have a very good idea, within the first two minutes, if the candidate is right for the job. Obviously, digging deeper for the right qualifications is necessary, but good demeanor, polish, eye contact, body language (expressions), the handshake, and straightforwardness are signs that people read right away.

I have always asked my assistant or the receptionist what they thought of the candidates in for interviews. If he or she impressed the person in this position, it is a good indication they will be able to *get past the gatekeeper* to connect with potential clients. Rude, condescending, or demanding candidates are screened right out of the process – since all organizations need team players.

There is a clear-cut way to make the interview process less stressful—to be prepared. Know the potential employer's business and exactly what the position you are applying for entails. When you are called or emailed to set up the interview, you shouldn't hesitate to ask for more details about the job (if needed). How will your skills contribute to the organization? You know better than anyone else what you are capable of and what you want out of a job. You will not be intimidated by questions or have your self-confidence shaken when you know the employer's needs and match them to your skills and strengths. Your confidence will be evident in the interview when you are prepared.

There are many ways to learn about the company. Pick up their annual report (if publicly traded), get information from their Web site and press releases, a business school library, and connect with some former employees through LinkedIn. Call the company and ask for information you feel is pertinent unless the job post states specifically – no calls. But you don't need to identify yourself. Many people will share information, if asked politely, to a person who says they are interested in working for the company. You might call unrelated departments, as a potential customer (everyone is a *potential* customer), and ask questions.

Your first interview with a company will usually be a screening interview by a human resources person or recruiter, which leads to the second interview if they feel you have the necessary qualifications. The trend today is to have 360-degree interviews with a panel of individuals, usually made up of the person whom you would report to, coworkers, people in other departments who interact with this position, and some of the people who would report to you. These may be separate interviews or all together. They are very demanding. Make sure you pay attention to everyone and every question asked. You cannot afford to alienate one person by focusing all of your attention on the prospective boss.

Then there is the interview with the boss's superior for his/her approval. This could very well be a lunch or dinner to get out of the office into a less formal setting. Obviously, politeness and table manners are important. My advice, and that given to every salesperson I have hired, is, "God gave you two ears and one mouth so that you will listen twice as much as you speak." You will be amazed at how much you discover about their background and additional things they are looking for in the prospective employee.

In *The 7 Habits of Highly Effective People,* Covey addresses the importance of listening skills.

> When another person speaks, we're usually 'listening' at one of four levels. We may be ignoring another person, not really listening at all. We may practice pretending. Yeah. Uh-huh. Right. We may practice selective listening, hearing only certain parts of the conversation. We often do this when we're listening to the constant chatter of a preschool child. Or we may even practice attentive listening, paying attention and focusing energy on

the words that are being said. But very few of us ever practice the fifth level, the highest form of listening, empathic listening. When I say empathic listening, I mean listening with intent to understand. I mean seeking first to understand, to really understand.

Empathic listening is so powerful, because it gives you accurate data to work with. Instead of projecting your own autobiography and assuming thoughts, feelings, motives and interpretation, you're dealing with the reality inside another person's head and heart.[28]

If you truly listen to understand the interviewer, he or she will give you more information than you thought possible. You can use this information and turn your skills into benefits useful to the company. In "salesmanship 101," you learn that buyers never buy because of the features of a product, only because of the *benefits*—benefits that fulfill a need the company may have. You must convey that you have the necessary skills to solve the company's needs. They surely have a need, or they wouldn't be interviewing and hiring. The trick is for you to find the particular needs relevant to the position—as not all are detailed in job descriptions.

Very few companies hire with only one or two interviews for more senior positions. Most likely, there will be third, four, and even fifth meetings. Being prepared is critical. You want to be consistent with the information you provide. They will be looking for any inconsistency. Ask questions about each of their jobs and backgrounds (there may be some connection from a past job or school). This will give you some control of the situation and feed their egos.

Avoid using "I" when possible in the interviews. Companies are looking for team players. Use "we were able to accomplish" this or that. A sales manager who says, "My sales team had over 20% sales increases in each of the three years since joining the company," is exhibiting leadership skill and giving the only legitimate form of self-praise. This gives you credibility while giving merit to your team—whom you hired and trained. It is much more impactful than anything you can say about yourself.

When you interview always carry your reference list with you, but don't offer the list unless asked. This list should be comprised of reputable people who you know will give you a positive reference. (You are usually asked for 3 to 5 references.) You must ask their permission prior to using them for this function and let them know each time they may expect a call. It is a good idea to discuss the job you are applying for with them, so that they can highlight your skills that pertain directly to the position. The most credible references will be from the industry you desire to enter and those with a high-level position in the field. This type of reference may not be attainable for you; I mention this as the optimum. Other leaders, such as a town councilman, priest, rabbi, coach, or professor, can also be effective as references for those with less tenure in the business world.

Part of being prepared is anticipating the questions you will be asked in an interview. Following are some general interview questions, which are fairly industry generic:

1.   Why did you leave your last position?
2.   Will your previous employer give you a good reference—or why not?
3.   In your last position, what were the most and the least enjoyable aspects?
4.   Considering the position you are applying for, what do you think it will take for a person to be successful?
5.   What are the specific strengths you will bring to this position?
6.   If you had to tell me what you were weakest at in your last position, what would that be?
7.   Describe a typical day at your current job.
8.   What would you like to be doing 5 years from now?
9.   Describe the best boss you ever had, and the worst.
10. What are your boss's title and responsibilities (current or previous)?
11. What might make your current boss more effective?

12. What is your most significant contribution since you've been in this type of work?
13. Describe your biggest failure and what you learned from it.
14. How do you go about handling a difficult personality?
15. Tell me about your style of management.
16. What do you want to know about our company?
17. What do you do in your free time? (This can be a tricky way to get you to answer some questions that are illegal to ask—such as, is this person religious, engaged in questionable activities, campaigning for a particular political party, etc.; so be prepared with some good solid citizen answers without going in a direction you don't want to go.)
18. What are the most important factors in selecting your next position, such as the company, commute, growth potential, salary, benefits, or hours?

The most prevalent question is the first one, why you left your last position. Be honest, but do not get into office politics or personality-clash discussions. There will be a big question as to your "fitting" into their culture or "political" environment. Do you have a personality type that frequently clashes with others? In these situations, simply say, "I felt it was time for me to move on—I had accomplished all I could in that company's organization." Or, "I felt I had more to offer (skills) than they gave me credit for—I was bottled up behind other people without my experience." This is as detailed as you want to be.

If it was a layoff or downsizing, say so. It could initiate the question of why were you let go instead of a coworker, unless it was a massive layoff. If you are confident in your abilities, I'd reply that senior management made across-the-board cuts without close examination of individual job performance. This happened in a frightening number of situations during the past recession. Many companies aren't experiencing all the positive results they anticipated from downsizing, and you might plant the seed that this was problematic in your former company. They are feeling pains at losing former employees like you—and other productive workers are leaving as a by-product.

Despite the fierce competition for jobs and promotions and ever-present specter of layoffs, downsizings, and bankruptcies, there is something positive working strongly in your favor. Employers still need employees. Someone has to do the job. That's why workers are the strongest assets a business has—and deep down, no matter how cavalier some employers are during times when jobs are scarce, they don't want you to leave. Regardless of how often you might be told that you can be easily replaced, it still takes time and money to do so.

A recent survey of 500 executives by InsightExpress, an online market research firm, shows that 59 percent of the top suits report they're worried that recent lay-offs will induce their remaining employees—the ones they kept because they are productive—to look for new jobs. "While employers have the upper hand in the job market today, they still need to pay attention to employee concerns," said Lee Smith, chief operating officer of the company. "When a key employee leaves, so do customers—and that's money out the door."[29]

One of the best answers for leaving a position is that you just completed a project (or annual sales objective) successfully and you are looking for more challenge and a broader base of experience. If you decide to leave your current employment, do so with an accomplishment under your belt. This will leave a better taste in the mouth of your previous employer, as well as be a positive calling card for the potential new one.

With the current flood of people into the job market, the pressure is stronger than ever for companies to find the right employees, with the most suitable skills. They have got to sort through a huge, competitive workforce— both employed and unemployed—to upgrade their labor force to remain competitive themselves as revenues (and profits) are under pressure. Recruiters have to search between the lines on resumes and during interviews to ensure they are taking advantage of the times, with an overabundance of potential employees in the market. This also means workers are under a greater deal of pressure, than they have been under in decades, to sell themselves to these potential employers. While you want to hone in on the job specifications, to demonstrate to the employer that you are *the one* for the job, you may also want to show your diverse skill set. If the employer is smart, they will hire people they can cross-utilize in the future. There is so much more cross-training of professionals these days, why not take advantage of the market and add these men and women to your ranks?

The key points employers want to see, in my opinion, are flexibility, skills mastered, work history indicating commitment, education and continuing education, diversity of interests, and someone who meets and exceeds goals set for them.

One of the greatest "cop-outs" you may hear is that you are "overqualified" for the position. The interpretation of this may just mean that the job applicant has more experience and higher degrees than the potential boss— something the ego-driven manager is not likely to handle well. I personally feel that some of these "overqualified" conversations amount to discrimination. Many times, people are kept out of jobs because of age or ethnic backgrounds, as well as the aspect of being a threat to a potential boss. If you are turned away for this reason, I suggest you contact the company's human resource department for an explanation. If you were brought in to meet or be interviewed by the boss's superior, you might follow up with a letter to him or her. With the relatively high percentage of unemployment in the country today, companies have an unprecedented opportunity to hire (more) qualified people. Senior management at most companies would like to know if the ego of one of their managers is blatantly getting in the way of a good hiring decision. Just be careful—avoid burning any bridges. That same company may have an opening you would be considered for at a later date.

If you are a more senior applicant, don't dwell on past accomplishments. You have got to convince the interviewer that you bring extraordinary value to the position. You must be up-to-date on the latest technology. Dress and look contemporary to leave a sharp, positive lasting impression. Discuss your outside activities: running, cycling, skiing, mountain climbing, tennis, or other activities that say you are energetic—without saying it!

The more confident you are about your abilities, the better you will come across in an interview. Write personal thank you notes to the top people you met with—use snail mail for delivery. E-mail will be okay for mass, 360-degree interviews, but make sure a handwritten, personal note goes to the potential boss(es). Get fully prepared for each interview opportunity and make each one count. You don't want to pass six interviews and get rejected on the seventh because you were not as primed as you should have been. Listen intently and ask leading questions. Listen some more, and let the interviewer sell herself on you.

CHAPTER 18

Negotiate for the Best Job Offer

There comes a point in negotiations when it becomes clear that both parties desire to do business with each other. A meeting of the minds is apparent – a surge of anticipation and mutual respect surfaces. I am referring to a win-win negotiation, where both parties seek to understand the other's point-of-view and perspectives. Stephen R. Covey conveys his thoughts on the subject:

> Win/win is a frame of mind and heart that constantly seeks mutual benefit in all human interactions. Win/ win means that agreements or solutions are mutually beneficial, mutually satisfying. With a win/win solution, parties feel good about the decision and feel committed to the action plan. Win/win sees life as a cooperative, not a competitive, arena. It's not your way or my way; it's a better way, a higher way.[30]

Employment negotiations are no different than any

other negotiations in business—only you are selling yourself, not someone's product or service. Companies typically base part of their managers' compensate on their ability to hold the line on costs. If the recruiting manager's perspective is that of maintaining a rigid, cost-conscious negotiation, without truly seeking to understand the candidate's ability and what she can contribute to the company, there is an inherent conflict. In effect, you have the potential for a win/lose situation. What the recruiter, in this scenario, may not understand is that if she underpays for your skill level, its only a matter of time before the realization hits that you are underpaid and dissatisfaction builds. Performance will suffer or you'll leave the organization altogether. What the employer thought was a win on their side suddenly becomes a loss. The same is true if you are overpaid for your position compared to the value you add to the company. Your boss will eventually start looking for fresh blood willing to work for less.

The "employee worth" discussion reinforces my conviction that compensation plans should include a base salary, which covers the basic cost of living, with productivity incentives that reward outstanding contribution. While this type of compensation has been widely utilized for sales positions, I think it has merit for other positions where output can be measured. There needs to be an ongoing review of the processes that make up the job to evaluate its necessity and what actual value is being added to the company's product or service. If an employee is living on the base pay and rarely earns incentive pay, he had better increase his contribution. In today's business climate, the company may replace him if complacency sets in.

One of the important reasons to network, and continuously examine the various opportunities unearthed, is so that you can gauge your worth—your market value. This will help you successfully negotiate with your existing employer or other companies in the future. If early on in negotiations you learn that a company has an inflexible compensation system, denying you the opportunity to reach your market value through salary, bonuses, and fringe benefits, you may want to walk.

Don't let your ego get in the way of a good opportunity, however. First, consider what the current market for jobs in your area (of expertise) is. Secondly, the career potential of the position must be weighed. Other factors, such as stock options, expenses, and 401(k) programs, must also be calculated. If you are placing yourself in the company's shoes and truly believe the position is one that is mutually advantageous, make a decision based on long-term considerations. When you weigh the impact of a higher tax rate on a higher salary, the increase you are seeking versus the salary the company is offering may not be an insurmountable difference.

I recommend the following type of response to the big question in employment negotiations. "What salary are you expecting to attain?" A good answer is, "Don't get me wrong, money is important and I'd like to earn as much as possible. But I'm more concerned about finding the best opportunity at this point in my life. I am very interested in this job and I am flexible regarding the salary. I am certain that you and your company will offer me a fair wage."

If you are sincere (the only way to be in these negotiations), you will come across as truly desiring a win/win relationship. You might even ask for a greater bonus potential (performance based) if the salary isn't where you feel it should be. This takes the risk out of the equation for the prospective employer. You win only if they win.

An extremely important consideration today is the strength of the company and the industry. As I have previously pointed out, there are no guarantees in the global economy of businesses surviving on their own, acquiring another, or being swallowed up by some other entity. But certain trends are evident and should be considered when making a decision to change jobs. There are regions of the country and career types that are definitely outperforming others. Check popular financial Web sites, like Bloomberg's, CNNMoney, or even the Commerce Department's Bureau of Labor Statistics, as this data will change with swings of our economy. The point is you need to think long and hard about switching to an industry that has little or no growth projected.

When you get a bona-fide job offer, negotiate from a position of knowledge. Knowledge is strength. Know your own skills backward and forward. Learn as much as possible about the company and the position you are interviewing for. Match your skills and their needs before salary is ever discussed. The winner in a negotiation is the side that has the most information and leverages it to their advantage. It's not personal between you and the person on the other side of the table. It's business, so don't show emotions—keep a poker face. Once they have made an offer, if it's not something you can accept let them know graciously. You will most likely want to tell them you need 24 or 48 hours to think it over. But if it's not what you need, decline the offer and thank them for the opportunity to explore the position. Don't come back with another figure—wait for the company's counter offer. You are the best judge of the situation and if the other party has room to negotiate on the "full" package. If you know they need your particular skills take a risk, but don't bluff unless you hold the "high cards" or you could get left out in the cold.

If you are running into a brick wall on salary negotiations, try to shift the focus back to their job description. Work on getting consensus that your skills (one by one) are really what they are looking for. But keep in mind they have already made the decision to hire you, so don't rehash all of the conversations to that point. If they are close on the compensation you need, and you believe this is the right company for you, try to get an agreement to review your salary earlier than their standard time frame.

Or perhaps get agreement for additional education at the company's expense. Most organizations realize this will benefit both you and them.

Never let yourself be pressured into accepting an offer. If you are dealing with reputable people, they will give you at least 48 hours to discuss the offer with a significant other, lawyer, accountant, or other confidante. Get the job offer in writing. There are many horror stories of individuals quitting other jobs only to find out that the company had put a hiring freeze in place, or the person offering the job did not have the authority to do so.

Carol Kleiman offers sound business advice: if an offer is made, get it in writing. "A written agreement from the employer delineates the new employee's responsibilities, hours, salary, benefits, to whom he reports, his expected starting time, vacation time, and other details that have been discussed with the employer. It serves the two-fold purpose of spelling out what's expected of the employee and of protecting him legally if the promised job disappears."[31]

An offer letter is fairly standard for any exempt position. It also protects the company from lawsuits brought about by someone thinking they were promised something different than what was actually offered. If the company will not write one, Carol Kleiman suggests that you write to the company and detail what you believe their offer to be. If there is any misunderstanding of the conditions of your employment, ask them to please let you know.

Employment contracts are rarely extended except to the most senior jobs or specialists. Most states have "employment at will" laws, and companies generally wish to retain the right to terminate employment at any time without cause. On shorter-term assignments or projects, I would definitely ask for an agreement with a start and end date, along with conditions.

A final note, never back someone into a corner in negotiations. "This is my bottom line—take it or leave it." Nine out of ten times, you will be left in the lurch. If the offer is not where it should be, ask whether it can be sweetened, i.e., "Please do what you can for me, I know you'll do your best. Then I'll make my decision." If you say no, do so amiably. You never know when or where you might bump into this person again. Thank them for their time and generous offer, but say you have to decline. You don't owe them details of your refusal or of any other offer. Simply say that the timing and/or compensation is not right at this juncture, perhaps we can work together sometime in the future.

CHAPTER 19

Make Your Move – Get A
New Job Or Promotion Now

We've pretty much hit rock bottom in the job market. Yes, some layoffs will continue in 2011 and beyond – there will always be downsizing – but the unemployment numbers will start dropping, as smart, well-managed companies have already begun to prepare for a sustained economic upturn. If you work for one of these forward thinking companies, you better start to jockey for position to replenish management ranks, as they bring new people on board to fill vacant and expansion positions held over from the deepest recession in decades.

This is similar to the wisdom imparted by a good stock market advisor, buy low and sell high. As we know in the market, many investors jump on the bandwagon trying to catch waves already cresting, then end up selling on the down slope. Companies have shed almost seven and one-half million jobs since the recession started, kept inventories at minimal levels, and stripped advertising budgets to the bone. They must now reposition themselves to take advantage of the economic upturn - even though the jobs piece of the equation is still on a somewhat slippery slope. This presents a great opportunity - in the trough of the jobs market - to advance in your career by riding the wave as recruitment begins in earnest.

Now is the time to gain maximum visibility in your company. Volunteer for new assignments, process improvement committees, to assist other departments, charity drives, even the holiday party planning team. Position yourself as the "go to" person in your department or division. Network within your company, with your manager, mentor, or any other connection, that you are ready for more responsibility. Update your resume and highlight your skills and experience, which have prepared you for more challenge. Why should your company's management look outside the organization, incur recruiting expenses, have questions if someone will fit into the company's culture, etc. when you are a proven asset? But it is up to you and your allies in the organization to communicate this. Your immediate boss, department manager, mentor(s), and others you interact with should be enlisted to sing your praises. Ask other departments, human resources, and your boss to keep you in the loop on jobs before they are even posted - to give you the first crack at them.

If your company does not have near term growth prospects for you, begin looking outside. Now is the time to re-evaluate your skills, education, and experience to begin the search for your dream job. Will you require some intermediate steps like going back to school for an MBA or other course work in your field? Do you need more experience in a particular discipline before you are qualified for your ultimate job? At the same time, evaluate if this dream job is in a field that is expected to continue to have above average growth in the coming years? Will it require a move to another part of the country? Do you have enough savings to make a move - since many companies have cut down on relocation reimbursements? All of these questions need to be answered as you take proactive steps to move forward down your career path.

If the chosen profession has limited growth and therefore upward movement, it may be time to look for a position in another field where your skills and experience will also apply. The US Labor Department has forecast the highest growth occupations through 2018, and may help you in your decision of where to look. Network systems and data communications positions will grow by over 53%; personal and home care aides by 50%; home health aides by almost 49%; computer software engineers by over 44%; and veterinary technologists by 41% to name a few. This information can be found, as well as fast growing cities, on the Bureau of Labor Statistics Web site.

A few words of caution - do not ignore any of your current job responsibilities as you look ahead, down your career path. And for heaven's sake don't tell co-workers you are looking elsewhere, as this will spread like wildfire and could damage chances for an internal promotion. Do your research away from the office, on your own computer and phone, and schedule interviews or meetings over lunch or take a vacation day.

It is up to you, and only you, to seize these new career opportunities, whether inside or outside of your current company. Timing is in your favor, as companies announce their expansion plans and flocks of transitional workers begin tossing their resumes into the hat. Go for it – don't delay!

CHAPTER 20

Career Success: Doing What You Love To Do

> "Do what you love to do and you will
> never work a day in your life."
> Confucius

To do something well, you most likely have to like doing it. Here is a recent post on a medical student/resident blog site: "Honestly, I don't even see being a doctor as a job, because it is such a great gift to be able to help and heal someone." I have also heard from some teachers who find teaching a real joy when they connect with difficult students—and see them fully grasp new concepts and exhibit a desire to learn. It has to be rewarding for a teacher. You also hear that firefighters, pastors, and even some airline pilots rank their jobs at the top of the "happiest" scale. Gurcharan Das, the Indian CEO for Proctor and Gamble, has been quoted on numerous occasions about what it is like to contribute all of your effort to the job at hand by being totally immersed in what you are doing. He says, "It is absorbedness—total contentment in work so engrossing that you don't even know that you are working. It may be working early morning hours without even realizing the time going by because you are so content in what you are doing."

The thought about doing the thing you most love to do, I believe presupposes a certain period of time. To eat a gourmet meal at a fine restaurant in Paris or sail around the Hawaiian Islands on a beautiful warm day (to most of us) is something we would love to do more than any job. So I think Confucius would agree that he meant what would give you the greatest satisfaction and pleasure over time – not for the moment.

I've known some graphic artists and programmers who say they love what they do and would never have to be asked to stay after 5 PM to finish a project. (Many would stay through the night if you bought the coffee). Most entrepreneurs and inventors get so caught up in what they are doing—totally immersed—that they lose sight of time, sleep, and even others who may not have the same passion.

Fund raisers for major charities, Peace Corp volunteers, veterinarians, ski instructors, actors, etc. have satisfying days but, I'm sure, also have ups and downs. The true test of whether someone loves what they do (his or her chosen profession) probably has to do with compensation. Would they be doing the same thing if they weren't making a decent wage doing so? Some attorneys do pro bono work for the disadvantaged or for the public good, but must have paying clients for their country club dues and house payments. An artist I know works on a particular painting for months without a chance of selling it for (much or any) profit, but that doesn't seem to discourage her. This must qualify for doing something you love. We could define "doing something you love to do for employment" as making a positive contribution – without starving to death.

In reality, you do not walk out the college doors and into the job of your dreams – one you will love, unless your love is raising horses and your family is ready hand over the reigns (pun intended) to the family ranch. If you have a passion about helping other people you might want to join a non-profit organization, start medical school, work for a political campaign, work for a homeless shelter, join the Peace Corp, etc. If you are a finance wiz, perhaps a job on Wall Street is your cup of tea, or working for one of the Big Four accounting firms. If you love travel and tourism, maybe American Express Travel, Expedia, American Airlines, or your state tourism department should be on your list. If you are a great cook, hair stylist, or florist and want to own your own restaurant, boutique shop, or franchise, there are skills you need to acquire to run a business (and be successful) no matter how much you love what you are doing. The point is that you are, in all probability, going to have to get an education, attain practical skills, and take intermediary steps to get to the point of doing what you love. Some of these steps may be drudgery but you've got to continuously look toward the end result.

Here's some practical advice I wholeheartedly agree with from Penelope Trunk, of Brazen Careerist. "Do not what you love; do what you *are*."[32] Many tests have been developed to highlight your strengths and weaknesses, such as Myers-Briggs, which provide a list of jobs where you would likely excel based on your strengths, experience, and education. Penelope goes on to say, "Relationships make your life great, not jobs. But a job can ruin your life – make you feel out of control in terms of your time or your ability to accomplish goals – but no job will make your life complete."[33]

Do what you love and perhaps money won't matter quite as much. In reality, by chasing the dream of what you love to do, you tap into an inner energy that propels you to do the best, most extraordinary work you are capable of. This will get you recognized and, if there is any money in your chosen field, you should be compensated accordingly.

To do something skillfully, you most likely have to like doing it – so consider a focus on what you "perform well" as your career. Concentrate on your strengths and immerse yourself in what you are doing. Contemplate the tough issues of where you have been, where you are now, and where you would like to be. Develop a (realistic) plan to get you there. Unless you are proactive, outline and complete the intermediate steps (and overcome the challenges), you won't end up where you want to be.

FOOTNOTES

1   Pausch, Randy. The Last Lecture. New York: Hyperion 2008.

2   Kleiman, Carol. Winning the Job Game. John Wiley & Sons. Hoboken, NJ 2002.

3   Friedman, Thomas L. The World Is Flat. Farrar, Straus, and Giroux. New York, NY. 2005

4   Kleiman, Carol. Winning the Job Game. John Wiley & Sons. Hoboken, NJ 2002.

5   Covey, Stephen R. The 7 Habits of Highly Effective People. New York: Fireside, 1990.

6   Hopkins, Tom. Bootstrap Business. Insight Publishing. Sevierville, TN, 2009

7   Connelly, Eileen Aj. The Associated Press. "Networking a neglected way to hunt down job leads."

The Denver Post. November 2, 2008.

8 Kawasaki, Guy. From: http://blog.guykawasaki. com/2009/02/10-ways-to-use.html#ixzz=06LdeSdKe

9 Corman, Steven R., Stephen P. Banks, Charles R. Bantz, and Michael E. Mayer. Foundations of Organizational Communication, 2nd ed. White Plains, NY: Longman Publishers, 1990.

10 Covey, Stephen R. The 7 Habits of Highly Effective People. New York: Fireside, 1990.

11 Britt, Robert Roy. "Job Insecurity Worse For Your Health Than Unemployment." LiveScience.com. August 28, 2009

12 Dahle, Cheryl. "Of Mentoring." Fast Company September 1998.

13 Kleiman, Carol. Winning the Job Game. John Wiley & Sons. Hoboken, NJ 2002.

14 Lindenberger, Judith. "Mentoring and Baby Boomers." www.lindenbergergroup.com 2010

15 Covey, Stephen R. The 7 Habits of Highly Effective People. New York: Fireside, 1990.

16 Kleiman, Carol. Winning the Job Game. John Wiley & Sons. Hoboken, NJ 2002.

17 Kleiman, Carol. *Ibid.*

18   Hammer, Michael and Steven A. Stanton. <u>The Reengineering Revolution</u>. New York: Harper Collins, 1995.

19   Hammer, Michael and Steven A. Stanton. *Ibid.*

20   Case, John. <u>Open Book Management: The Coming Business Revolution</u>. New York: Harper Business 1995.

21   Kleiman, Carol. <u>Winning the Job Game</u>. John Wiley & Sons. Hoboken, NJ 2002.

22   Handy, Charles. <u>The Age of Unreason</u>. Boston, MA: Harvard Business School Publishing 1998.

23   Sokoloshy, Valerie. "How To Be a Valued Employee." Spirit Southwest Airlines magazine July 1998.

24   US Department of Labor, http://www.bls.gov 2011

25   Britt, Robert Roy. "Job Insecurity Worse For Your Health Than Unemployment." LiveScience.com. August 28, 2009

26   Kleiman, Carol. <u>Winning the Job Game</u>. John Wiley & Sons. Hoboken, NJ 2002.

27   Kleiman, Carol. *Ibid.*

28   Covey, Stephen R. <u>The 7 Habits of Highly Effective People</u>. New York: Fireside, 1990.

29   Kleiman, Carol. <u>Winning the Job Game</u>. John Wiley & Sons. Hoboken, NJ 2002.

30   Covey, Stephen R. <u>The 7 Habits of Highly Effective People</u>. New York: Fireside, 1990.

31   Kleiman, Carol. <u>Winning the Job Game</u>. John Wiley & Sons. Hoboken, NJ 2002.

32   Trunk, Penelope. "Bad career advice: Do what you love." BrazenCareerist.com December 2007.

33   Trunk, Penelope. *Ibid.*

21.95

CPSIA information can be obtained at www.ICGtesting.com
Printed in the USA
LVOW111534290212

271003LV00003B/55/P

9 781432 741372